Releasing Heaven's Song

Singing Over Your Nation for Breakthrough and Revival

Roma Waterman

© Copyright 2013, Roma Waterman

All materials contained in this book are the copyrighted property of Roma Waterman. To reproduce, republish, post, modify, distribute or display material from this publication, you must first obtain written permission from the author at:

Roma Waterman
P O Box 825
Ringwood Victoria
Melbourne, Australia 3134
roma@romawaterman.com
www.romawaterman.com

Published and distributed by: I Was Carried Pty Ltd, Melbourne Australia

Cover Design by Paul Wayland Lee

ISBN-13: 978-1482025774
ISBN-10: 1482025779

Endorsements

As a musician and songwriter in the church, I have read many books and exhaustively researched from vast sources in regards to the broad spectrum of praise and worship... but when I began to read Roma Waterman's "Releasing Heaven's Song" what I uncovered was a book that stood out far above the rest! I believe that this strategic handbook will be used by thousands around the world to usher in a new realm of God's Spirit within church congregations, cities, and nations as they discover the simple yet powerful dimension of singing the New Song. Several years ago the Lord spoke to me and said, "Every new day comes with a new song and every new song brings forth a new realm of Glory." This revelation from heaven urged me to begin exploring this often uncharted realm of the unknown. Within the pages of this revelatory treasure you will explore this sound and atmosphere which produces dynamic breakthrough and releases victories in your home and among the multitudes. This book not only contains excellent scriptural and practical understanding, but it also carries an invitation into heavenly encounters that will radically change your world. I love this book and I will be using it myself as I teach the Nations to sing a new song that brings Revival and Glory.

Joshua Mills
Recording Artist, Prophetic Minister & Bestselling Author, New Wine International, Inc. / The Intensified Glory Institute®, Vancouver, Canada / Palm Springs, California, www.JoshuaMills.com

If I were to compose a list of today's top trainers in the area of prophetic worship one name you would be sure to see is Roma Waterman. Roma's woven depth of experience as a touring contemporary musical artist, a conference speaker and a devoted servant of the local church empowers her tested principles to be as effective in the marketplace as they are in the secret place.

The prophetic is simply God revealing (in any specific area) the treasures of wisdom and knowledge that are hidden in the person of Jesus Christ. When we sing what God Himself is saying then the very fabric of the Universe responds to the sound of the voice that created it. This foundational concept stands as true for microscopic protoplasmic particles as it does for mega-planets, galaxies and star systems. With this fundamental understanding, singing over cities, regions and nations is not only powerfully prophetic but intensely practical and essential to releasing God's purposes in the earth. Roma's book entrusts and empowers the readers with these secrets of this heavenly reality.

Dan McCollam
Faculty of Bethel School of Supernatural Worship, WorshipU instructor, International Director of Sounds of the Nations missions organization, author of *Basic Training for Prophetic Activation*, *God Vibrations* and *Finding Your Song*.

My friend Roma is one of the true Pioneers of the worship movement in Australia. Her new book "Releasing Heaven's Song" is awesome! If you are a singer, musician, worship leader, psalmist, or if you just love to worship and are looking to go to the next level, then this is the very tool that will help take you there!

Rick Pino
Fire Rain Ministries

God created us to be image-bearing worshippers who carry His song from nation to nation and land to land; tribe to tribe and tongue to tongue. Don't overlook the kitchen and living room. Thank you Roma for all the amazing revelation and practical truth. I especially love the way that you demystify the process and help us carry and release heaven's song.

Ray Hughes
Selah Ministries
Author, speaker, musician

What a debt we owe to the prophetic minstrels who have been honing their craft in the secret place so that the wider church become the beneficiaries of their prophetic encounters with the heart of God. Roma is a great Australian pioneer who has pressed into the heart of the Father as a passionate worshipper and has accessed something so profound that it releases the sounds of heaven on earth. Supernatural power is released through the prophetic song as it touches and unlocks the heart in ways that words alone cannot. I strongly recommend this training manual for all those who recognize the potential of prophetic songs to shift the church into the fullness of revival culture. Worshippers are the true pioneers of the heart journey leading us to the infinite love of our Father. Follow Roma as she guides you on the ultimate heart journey into intimacy with God's heart through the power of the heavenly song. In our own worshipping community every time we gather I delight in following the worshippers into the glory realm. Follow the worshippers and your heart will stay tender before the Lord!

Phil Mason
Spiritual Director, New Earth Tribe
Byron Bay, Australia

Roma Waterman's love for song, people and the heart of God comes through so passionately in this book. She is a pioneer forging new ground for others to follow in and has both taught and demonstrated the prophetic in song over many years. As a worship leader in our Stairway community Roma has inspired people across the generations to trust God to release His words through their creative gifts. Her revelations and practical tips allow new realms to open up in song that carry life and breakthrough. This book will give you fresh inspiration and a great biblical grounding for the prophetic in your worship. Release the song!

Ursula Cettolin
Worship and Creative Arts Pastor
Stairway Church Whitehorse, Melbourne, Australia

God's presence is permeating and resonating throughout the heavens and the earth and globally He is calling a generation to tune into the frequency of His voice and rise up in their destiny to declare His words with power and authority, in turn releasing the fullness of His presence. "Releasing Heaven's Song" by Roma Waterman is the "how to manual" that is the result of her life's journey persistently pursuing God's heart and truth for worship and the life of the worshipper. In a culture of ever increasing passing fads, Roma focuses the reader on God's eternal instructions and energizes their creativity with numerous practical examples and exercises in a beautiful atmosphere of freedom and encouragement. I highly recommend not only reading but living out "Releasing Heaven's Song."

Derek Bailey
Producer, Singer / songwriter
Visit www.derekbailey.com for info on his soaking album *Never Alone*

Not only have I had the pleasure of reading this workbook, I have also had the joy of watching Roma teach these tools to some our worship team here at The Rock of Roseville (CA). The principles found in "Releasing Heaven's Song" are both transformative and enabling. I found myself wishing that I had this workbook years ago! Roma is not just giving you ideas, she is giving you practical advice that has come from what she has experienced over years of leading worship and singing Heaven's song. You will not regret having this tool in your hands.

Ben Woodward
Singer/Songwriter, Worship Pastor and lover of Jesus, USA

Every pastor needs to read this to help them empower the worship leader to sing heaven's song. Every worship leader needs to read this to help them empower their church to sing heaven's song. Every Christian needs to read this book to learn how to sing heaven's song.

Roma Waterman has put together a master class that breaks down why and how we sing the song of heaven in a practical tool for every church. It's easy to read, broken down into almost a workshop environment that a worship team could easily work and grow through together. Having been personally mentored by Roma for fifteen years I can't recommend her enough. Her wisdom and her prophetic insight have spoken directly into my life more than even Roma knows. Her heart to see the church worshipping in unity is inspiring and will inspire you to sing your song of heaven.

Judd Field
Singer-Songwriter, Choir Director of the Melbourne Gospel Choir, Worship Leader at City life Church Melbourne.

Acknowledgements

Thank you to my friend Dan McCollam. Your mentoring and training is indelibly printed on my heart and on the pages of this book. Thanks for taking time to help me grow into what God has called me to be. I am deeply grateful.

Special thanks to Lisa Veness and Amrit Kleingeld for proof reading. And special thanks to my assistant Sarah Camez, management consultant Anton Bekker, and everyone in Sounds of the Nations Oceania and abroad, including Paul Wayland Lee for amazing artwork and help, and for adding a little humor!

As always, love and appreciation for my wonderful and amazing family. My husband Ted, and children Angel and Asa. I'm so blessed to be wife and mother to this tribe.

TABLE OF CONTENTS

Introduction

What is the New Song? 13

What Heaven's Song Can Achieve 31

HOW TO RELEASE HEAVEN'S SONG: Singing What You See 47

HOW TO RELEASE HEAVEN'S SONG: Singing What You Dream 57

HOW TO RELEASE HEAVEN'S SONG: Singing Prophetic Words 65

HOW TO RELEASE HEAVEN'S SONG: Singing Scripture 75

HOW TO RELEASE HEAVEN'S SONG: Singing What You Feel 85

Your Prophetic Identity as a Worshipper 107

What to do When you Don't Know What to do 123

Different Expressions of Heaven's Song 139

How to Turn Spontaneous Songs into Structured Songs 159

Cultivating an Atmosphere That Releases Heaven's Song 175

Conclusion 201

Introduction

Releasing Heaven's Song is a workbook designed to:

- Teach you how to release the song of the Lord in your region in your own authentic sound;

- Provide strategy, understanding, and leverage points to help you have influence and breakthrough in your nation and region;

- Teach you how to release that song not only in a corporate setting, but also in your own personal worship time.

Whether spontaneous or structured, heaven's song is waiting to be released through you.

As we draw closer to Him, let us become more mindful of what that song sounds like and how it can be expressed. When we become intentional about what the Lord can release to and through us, a song becomes more than a song. The melody carries power and breakthrough.

Every time I worship, I expect encounter. As a worshipper and a songwriter, that is only going to happen if I am intentional about hearing and releasing heaven's song.

The spontaneous song is not just for a certain denomination, a certain church group, or even just for a Sunday service. It will look different in different settings, but it is ready and available for all who desire it. Much like a preacher will have notes off a page to read yet expand thoughts and create a conversation as he is speaking, we can also do this with song. People pray from their heart and it's completely acceptable. Singing the spontaneous song is praying from your heart – with melody!

I pray that the ideas found within these pages will be a starting point for you to develop your own authentic style. I am not trying to provide you with a formula but rather ideas that will inspire passion in you to release heaven's kingdom through worship. I pray that it catapults you into all the Lord has waiting for you.

WHAT IS THE NEW SONG?

Something fresh and new

Psalm 96:1 NIV
*"Sing to the LORD a **new song**;*
sing to the LORD, all the earth."

The word new in this verse is the Hebrew word *"chadash"* which means *"new"* and *"fresh."* [1]

The root word also infers something that is *"restored," "repaired"* (from the Hebrew word *"piel"*) and to *"repair oneself"* (from the Hebrew word *"hithpael"*). [2]

This infers that we are commanded to sing the song that:

---

[1] *Strong's Concordance* – H2319 – www.blueletterbible.org
[2] *Strong's Concordance* – H2318 – www.blueletterbible.org

- Is new and fresh.
- Brings restoration and repair.
- Brings healing to ourselves.

I also love these two thoughts from the *Gesenius Lexicon* describing the Biblical usage of the word "new":

> *"... Etymologists have well observed that its primary sense is that of cutting and polishing ... the significance of newness appears to proceed from that of a sharp polished splendid sword."*

and:

> *"PIEL – to renew ... especially to repair or restore buildings or towns"*

From these implications we can assume that the new song is:

- Forged, cut and polished – it is well written, or presented well;
- Sharp – it reaches the target it is designed for and cuts through the hardest of hearts;
- Splendid – it is beautiful in nature – it is a work of art.

The reason that the new song is so powerful is because it can be many things at the same time. It is fresh, new, yet it is also a repaired and restored sound. It can be something that is spontaneous, yet it also can be a structured song. Both have been inspired from the Holy Spirit. It is a sound that is fresh and exciting but at the same time can also sound familiar or sound like "home." It can be a song written and released for the right moment in time, yet be sung one hundred years later, much like the hymns of Charles or John Wesley and still be relevant and fresh.

Don't underestimate the power of the new song and what it can do in the hearts of people and yourself. Don't dismiss something because it is old or has been "done before," yet at the same time, don't dismiss that which is new and unfamiliar. The new song is everywhere and ready for all who have ears to hear and mouths to sing.

A song everyone can sing

The other part of Psalm 96:1 I like is the phrase *"all the earth."* *The Treasury of David* so aptly explains it when it states:

> *"National jealousies are dead; a Jew invites the Gentiles to adore and joins with them, so that all the earth may*

lift up one common psalm as with one heart and voice unto Jehovah, who hath visited it with his salvation."[3]

We can gather from this explanation that the new song is a song that's not just for the church, it's a song that everyone that wants to know Christ can sing. It's not just something for the "in crowd," or a certain denomination or age group. Everyone is included.

If we think the new song is only for a Sunday church service, we are limiting the power of it. Our culture has somewhat confined the sound of heaven to corporate church settings, or a certain songwriter, or a certain artist. This is so sad. The new song is much bigger than a song service or a flavor.

I still remember the first time we sang backing vocals on national TV for an artist. Here in Australia, *Carols by Candlelight* is a TV program that airs on Christmas Eve all over Australia and to over 56 countries, reaching around 20 million people. It was a dream and to be honest an absolute miracle to be asked to sing on this show and over the span of te" or so years we have been blessed to do so many times.

The first year we performed on this TV show, it was to sing "O Happy Day." I will never forget the feeling of walking out

---

[3] National Treasury of David

on stage to thousands of candles glowing in the evening light. Here we were, a bunch of "church singers," singing "when Jesus washed my sins away" to thousands of people at a venue, and to millions of people worldwide. As we did so, everyone was singing along. It was a surreal moment.

Before we went on stage, we prayed that those words would pierce the heart of everyone hearing them. When I began to sing, I was choking back tears as I felt the presence of God so strong in those three minutes of live television. It was a powerful moment – yet one we could have missed if I had assumed heaven's song was just to be released in a church service.

Where is heaven's song waiting to be released through you?

It represents unity/inclusivity

It's also a song that is "unanimous" – if it's a song the *whole earth* can sing. This could represent unity, people being of one mind.

Makes people see

Psalm 40:3 NIV

"He put a new song in my mouth, a hymn of praise to our God. Many will see and fear and put their trust in the LORD."

When you sing the new song, it's not just about people *hearing* it. This scripture says when you sing, people will *see*! There are many songs, even worship songs that are pleasing to the ear – they sound nice and they are written well. However the new song is bigger than that, it helps people *see* the Lord. What an amazing thought – that when you release the new song, people not only hear but they see and put their trust in the Lord.

It is skillful

Psalm 33:3 NIV

"Sing to him a new song; play skillfully and shout for joy."

We are commanded to not only sing something new, but also be skillful about it. I love this. Most people think that to flow with the Holy Spirit means doing whatever we want, singing out of key, and not worrying about how well we play our instrument. Of course, the Lord loves the authentic praises of our heart but as musical people we must also be mindful of becoming skilled in what we do. Don't use His love for us as an excuse not to become more disciplined in the gifts He has given us.

I have noticed in prophetic circles that this discipline is often overlooked or not deemed as important. I have even had people say to me, "I just want to move with the Spirit, I don't need to learn all the rules."

This saddens me because this is not a scriptural paradigm. King David only used the best musicians to worship in the temple. For them to be the best they had to be skilled. In fact, they were not only called "artists" but "artisans," which implies someone who is the best in their chosen field.

David knew giving the best was a good and acceptable offering to the Lord. It has been said by many that David himself invented and was skillful on many instruments:

Amos 6:5 ESV
"...and like David invent for themselves instruments of music..."

To have that capacity he needed to be skillful and strategic.

If David – one of the greatest worshippers who ever lived, a man who God says was a man after his own heart – was like this, then why would we think we do not need to be?

Here's an example: In King Solomon's temple, according to music historian Abraham Schwadron, there was a *"high degree of musico-liturgical organization ... such as the 24 choral groups consisting of 288 musicians which took part in 21 weekly services."*[4] That's a lot of services and a lot of work! You need to be skillful not only to minister like this but also to manage something like this.

You have probably heard that phrase "the more you know the less you know." This is true, but what is also true is that the more you know, the more capacity you are able to have. By being skillful we are not lessening the value of moving with the Holy Spirit. We are actually engaging it, proving ourselves worthy, ready, and *hungry* to be filled by God for His song to spill out from us.

It also provides a platform where it is easier to move in the prophetic because we don't have to concern ourselves as much with all the technical aspects of musicality. Personally

---

[4]Schwadron, Abraham A. *Music of Many Cultures: An Introduction*, Ch. 16. Univ. of California Press (1983)

I believe there is nothing more powerful than a skilled musician who is ready to move with the Holy Spirit.

SUMMARY – WHAT IS THE NEW SONG?

1. A fresh, new, restored or repaired sound.

2. Brings healing to ourselves.

3. Is forged, sharp polished and splendid like the finest sword.

4. A song that everyone can sing – not just the church.

5. A song that brings unity/draws people together.

6. A song that not only makes people hear but makes people see.

7. Is skillful.

ACTIONS

1. What is an example of a song that everyone can sing, not just the church? (It could be a worship song or a pop song – you choose!)

2. What is an example of a song that brings unity and draws people together?

3. What is an example of a song that not only makes people hear but makes people see? How does it do this? Is it by imagery? Melody? Is it the person singing/playing it?

4. What are the ingredients in these types of songs that you could include in your own singing or songwriting? List at least three.

5. What is an area in your life as a worshipper that could require a greater discipline? Write down what this is. Next to it, write down an action plan – what do you need to do to improve in this area? Finally, write down a time frame of when you would like to achieve this. Don't feel tied to this time frame but give yourself something to work towards.

Chapter Two

Why Sing the New Song?

It is a command

First, it's a command in scripture. We are urged and encouraged in many scriptures to sing to Him:

Psalm 98:1 NIV
"Sing to the LORD a new song, for he has done marvelous things; his right hand and His holy arm have worked salvation for him."

He has done marvelous things

We sing because He has done wonderful things, as mentioned in the above scripture.

It is encouraging and prophetic

Ephesians 5:19 NIV
"Speak to one another with psalms, hymns and spiritual songs. Sing and make music in your heart to the Lord."

What does the term "spiritual songs" infer? The *Commentary Critical and Explanatory on the Whole Bible* says it like this:

> *"the general term for lyric pieces; 'spiritual' is added to mark their being here restricted to sacred subjects, though not merely to direct praises of God but also containing exhortations, prophecies."*[5]

We can see from this study that part of the way we bring glory to God is not just to sing praises to Him but to encourage and prophesy in spiritual song. The new song encourages and prophesies.

It is an appropriate emotional response

Singing is an emotional response to something felt deeply in the heart. Becoming so moved by all Christ has done for us, worship bubbles up inside and needs to flow out somehow. If you think about it, most songs that have had an impact on the world have an emotional attachment to them. It's either happy, sad, or angry. The same is true for our worship – we sing from an emotional response, an overflow of the heart. Many commentaries state that when the scriptures relate to

---

[5] *Commentary Critical and Explanatory on the Whole Bible.* This one volume commentary was prepared by Robert Jamieson, A. R. Fausset and David Brown and published in 1871. *Commentary Critical and Explanatory on the Whole Bible* is in the public domain and may be freely used and distributed.

singing a new song, it is meant to be a heartfelt response, not just words or head knowledge.

SUMMARY – WHY SING THE NEW SONG?

1. It is a command.

2. He has done wonderful things.

3. It encourages and releases the prophetic.

4. It is a response to how deeply we feel about what God has done for us.

ACTIONS

1. Think about something in your life or church that needs to be repaired or broken. What structured songs speak into that situation?

2. Write down in point form what type of song would bring a refreshing. For example if there are people dear to you who are very sick, you may write down "a song of healing." Or you could even be more specific – if you feel the Lord highlighting healing from cancer, you may write "blood cells regenerating." If there is divorce, it may be "a song of love, forgiveness and grace."

3. Are there songs you know of that you are not currently singing that could be included in your corporate and private worship time? List them.

4. If you were going to release a song over that situation – what words would you use that would bring restoration and healing? Write down ten words.

5. This week, aim to sing one or two of those songs regularly in your quiet time with God, in your

rehearsal time or in your corporate worship services. Observe if there is a shift in the atmosphere.

Chapter Three

WHAT HEAVEN'S SONG CAN ACHIEVE

Releasing heaven's song is vital to the growth of the church, revival, and awakening. If you study church history, you will notice that every revival had a sound attached to it. Billy Graham had Ira Sankey, John Wesley had Charles Wesley. More modern day examples are movements like Jesus Culture, The RAMP, and others. Worship was and is vital to every move of God.

Here are some of the things I believe the song of the Lord can achieve.

Bringing heaven to Earth
When you sing out what heaven wants to release, you create opportunities for the physical realm to be invaded by the spiritual realm.

The best way I can describe it is by explaining it in picture form. This is not a technical or scientific explanation by any means, but it is a way to help you understand the importance of your song.

Imagine there is a frequency vibrating in the heavens. It is above the earth – but separate from the earth. I see this as a line that is vibrating up and down – constantly moving and creating waveforms. In this frequency, anyone that "steps into it" can access the healing of God and experience His love, peace and joy. There is also enormous revelation here. Anyone that experiences this vibration experiences everything heaven wants to release.

Now imagine there is a frequency vibrating over the earth. It looks the same as the first frequency but carries different "sounds" to it. It carries depression, despair, confusion, sickness and disease. Imagine that people are walking to and fro going about their daily activities and they keep "stepping in" to this frequency. It's everywhere, it's common, and it's easy to walk into it without even realizing it.

Then imagine that if heaven's frequency was something tangible, something that could be touched or felt, that someone is reaching with their hands up into the heavens and pulling down heaven's frequency into the earthly realm. As they do this, the earth's frequency becomes the weaker sound. In fact, Earth's frequency is so weak, that when heaven's vibration comes close to it, the earth's frequency begins to align itself with heaven. It has no choice but to surrender to the stronger frequency. *This is the "Principle of Entrainment" in action: vibrations that are similar in nature will eventually align themselves to the stronger vibration.* [6]

When you sing heaven's song, you are releasing heaven's frequency. You are calling heaven to Earth. You are partnering with the divine. Another way to think of it is that you are releasing a portal where Earth can partake in all that heaven would want to release to us.

Releases revelation and understanding

Releasing heaven's song reveals who God is. We have already discussed in previous chapters that the new song is more than just something people can hear – it helps people see.

---

[6] The principle of entrainment is explained in depth in my book *The God Artist: The Quest for Supernatural Creative Influence.*

A practical explanation of this is that it can reveal things to others that were previously hidden. Heaven's song brings revelation and understanding. It helps people experience the Love of God. It helps people see things from heaven's perspective. It takes the blindfold off our eyes. Again, this is really the principle of entrainment in action.

Releases healing and breakthrough

Because heaven's song is releasing heaven to Earth, all that heaven has to offer can be released when it is sung out. I have been in many meetings where I have felt I was to sing out to release healing. I have heard countless stories of people being healed as they worship, because heaven's song releases that into the atmosphere. I am energized by the thought that just by being in God's presence, we can experience healing.

It gathers people

The sound of heaven gathers people together. I love the story of when those in the Upper Room were filled with the Holy Spirit:

Acts 2:1-8 NIV
*[1] "When the day of Pentecost came, they were all together in one place. [2] Suddenly **a sound** like the blowing of a violent*

wind came from heaven and filled the whole house where they were sitting. ³ They saw what seemed to be tongues of fire that separated and came to rest on each of them. ⁴ All of them were filled with the Holy Spirit and began to speak in other tongues as the Spirit enabled them. ⁵ Now there were staying in Jerusalem God-fearing Jews from every nation under heaven. ⁶ **When they heard this sound,** *a crowd came together in bewilderment, because each one heard them speaking in his own language. ⁷ Utterly amazed, they asked: 'Are not all these men who are speaking Galileans? ⁸ Then how is it that each of us hears them in his own native language?'"*

Reminds people who God is

Keep in mind heaven's song is both the structured song and the spontaneous song we can sing that reminds the congregation/listener of who God is. Heaven's song is that which is breathed upon by God.

I know it seems impossible that we could forget who God is, but the truth is the things of this world are at war against us drawing closer to God. There are so many things that try to pull us away from His presence. It is so subtle, too; we can often be experiencing depression, confusion, stress, and anxiety and not realize how we got there!

When I hear heaven's song, I experience the feeling of being centered. I like to call it an "ah ha!" moment – the moment when I remember that God is God and controls, conquers, and comforts. A minute under the influence of heaven's song can unravel months of disillusionment and disappointment.

We duplicate heaven's song

You can sing out something spontaneously that a congregation can sing along to – and the power of that is you are helping people sing out heaven's song as well. As we worship, we are also equipping people with heaven's song for themselves. We are duplicating the song so that it is being released by many. This is so powerful.

I have a friend who pastors a church where the worship is mainly spontaneous. The first time I went there I kept looking up at the screen to find the words. After about ten minutes and no words, I realized she was singing spontaneously. However it was so simple and easy to follow that the congregation was able to follow her wherever she went. So as she was being led by the Spirit, so was the congregation. Heaven's song was being released, then being duplicated. That is powerful!

Helps us remember the word of God

Singing songs that have good theology is one of the best ways to learn the scriptures and who God is. One of my concerns about the prophetic song is that because we are singing from our heart, we think we can sing whatever we want. Of course, the overflow of the heart is important; that spontaneous sound bubbling up from the core of who we are is the song God loves because it is authentic and real.

If we are studying the word and letting it dwell in us, we will naturally be aligning ourselves with good theology. I find it sad that Christian musicians are not known for their knowledge of the scriptures. There is sometimes the expectation that it is the preacher who delivers the word from God and it's the worshippers who just sing about how wonderful He is.

We have a responsibility to learn all we can so that we can transfer that to those we are leading! We are leading people into His presence! If we don't understand what we are doing we won't be leading them very well. If you think about it, there are not many sermons people remember that are over 100 years old but we are singing hymns that are older than that.

Brings strategy

When the Israelites went to war, it was always the singers and musicians that went first. This dumbfounded the enemy as they were met with singing and celebration to the King of Kings. It's not the first thing you would expect in a battle! But this also indicates that to release the song of the Lord, you were considered a *worship warrior.* You were part of the army. To be part of an army, you not only need to be bold but you need to be strategic. You need to have knowledge of the battle.

Where the song of the Lord is most effective

The song of the Lord is not always for church. If this is the only forum you feel it can be expressed you will quickly become frustrated. It must be bigger than a service.

Here are some examples in my own life where I have sung a prophetic song outside of a church setting:

Café

I used to sing in a café on Sunday afternoons. While people were eating I would sit at the piano and go through a list of well-known cover songs. I was really doing it because I needed the money and found it so difficult because I did not feel I was worshipping. One day the Lord challenged me on my attitude. He said to me: *"What would it look like if you began to sing prophetically during your set?"*

Every now and then, at the end of a well-known song I would continue playing in the same key and begin to just make up a song on the spot. It was so much fun and I could sense a shift in the atmosphere as I did this. I would just sing whatever came to mind/what was on my heart. I began to look forward to those moments, as I began to understand many of these people would probably never walk into a church.

Television

Sometimes before we have performed on TV as the Melbourne Gospel Choir, we have had a prayer time in our dressing room and we will sing a song together to end our prayer time. One particular time we were doing this, after a few minutes a celebrity who was also performing that evening was standing at our door. This person said, "I hope you don't mind but I was in my dressing room by myself and I heard your singing. Do you mind if I join you?" Now this person was not a Christian but *heard the sound* of worship backstage before a TV gig and came to join in. This is someone who has probably never walked into a church!

There have also been many times when we have laid hands on people backstage and just began to sing over them. Often because they know we are believers they will ask us to pray for them. This is the perfect time to sing over them and it's not uncomfortable because they are often singers themselves. We have so many stories of people encountering God during these times.

One thing I have become more aware of is that we think it's unusual to do this, but most unbelievers don't. If you step out and release heaven's song, you will be quite surprised at how accepted it will be by those around you. This is because everyone wants to experience God. Everyone wants proof that He exists and He cares for them. What better way to release that than by singing a song straight from heaven!

Taxi

I remember a journey from Sydney airport up into the blue mountains of New South Wales. In our taxi was a woman who was coming to the conference I was a guest speaker at. This person was invited by her friend and was not a Christian. The drive was a couple of hours and we began talking. After a while, she asked if I would sing over her. So

I sang over her right in that taxi. It was such a joy to see her moved by God's presence as she received from Him.

Private dining room

I was once asked to be part of a private dinner at a fancy restaurant with a few celebrities. I really don't know how I got invited and what I was doing there! There were people from all different streams of the entertainment industry: there was boxing champion, a TV host, record producers and the like. As I was sitting there, the Lord was giving me great compassion for these people. Finally, they asked me what I did for a living. Once I told them that I sang, they asked me to sing something right then and there. It felt strange and I was a little nervous but the first song that came into my head was "Amazing Grace," so I began to sing it over them. When I finished singing it was such a privilege to feel God's presence enter the room in the form of great love for them. These experiences really help me understand what is going on in the heart of people. God loves people so much.

Your song is important

I am not sharing these stories because I am anybody special or think I have talents better than anyone else. I don't think I am the best singer around – there are heaps of people more talented than I am. I share these stories to encourage you – if you just trust that God can use you and that the song that is in your heart is important, you will release something bigger than yourself. Don't think what you have inside of you is not important. All it takes is for you to be bold and you will surprise yourself. The more you step out, the stronger it will become.

If I had assumed heaven's song was only to be released in a church setting I would missed some amazing opportunities. In fact, there are sometimes limitations to releasing it in this arena. This is why it's important to experiment but also to spend time at home alone expressing your heart to Him. With the freedom to make mistakes, we find room to explore the boundaries of our gifts in greater measure.

Secret place worship
Singing in the secret place before it reaches the market place – spending time with the Lord away from the crowd is so important. When I was worship pastor at my church, we were asked to do an exercise to see how much time we were spending doing what. We were asked to write down what we do and in percentage form, how much time we spent doing it. I was quite shocked to note after this exercise that a majority of my time was spent on the platform. It was around 80%. This was a great concern to me. I was

spending more time worshipping the Lord on a stage, than I was in the secret place. I was spending more time leading, and less time writing songs, praying and reading my Bible. These things still happened but it was a little out of balance.

I had to make some big changes to rectify this. I knew that if I continued down this road I could still have a successful public ministry, but at what cost? The anointing would still be on my life and it would appear to people that I was working in my gift but I knew in my heart that I was not spending most of my ministry time alone with the Father. That is where the power and the peace are. I realized for the season I was in, for me to achieve this change, it would mean stepping down as the worship pastor. It was not easy to make this decision but I feel I have become a better worship leader and am more effective in my church because I am spending more time in the throne room than in the auditorium. Now, the bulk of my time is spent worshipping at home in my studio. It is wonderful, refreshing and the best of me comes out in public when I do this.

If the only time you are releasing the spontaneous song is in a public service, you will not develop and grow. You need space to make mistakes, free flow without time constraints, to cry and to reach out.

My album *Release the Sound* is made up of songs that were written during these private worship times. I would sit at my piano without an agenda. It was my devotional time with the Lord. I didn't go in there with the intention of writing a song. I went to the piano with the intention of honoring the Lord with a song. As I began to do this, I was amazed at how many songs were flowing out of me. The whole album is really snippets of moments where a line would pour out and then eventually I would turn it into a song. You will be amazed at what will flow into you and then flow out of you when you spend time like this with God.

SUMMARY – What Heaven's Song Can Achieve

1. Brings Heaven to Earth.
2. Releases Revelation and understanding.
3. Releases healing and breakthrough.
4. Gathers people.
5. Reminds people who God is.
6. Can be duplicated.
7. Helps us remember the word of God.
8. Brings strategy.
9. Heaven's song can be released in more settings than just a church service.
10. Your song is important.
11. Heaven's song is found in the secret place.

ACTIONS

1. What strategies can you obtain to release the song of the Lord? Write them down. It could be to improve as a songwriter, to learn a scripture every day or study the word.

2. You are probably wondering how it will be possible to release heaven's song in a setting aside from church. A lot of times it isn't happening because we are not looking for it outside of a church service. Begin to look with new eyes this week and see if there is a moment where your song could be appropriate. Step out and be bold. It might be a few lines or it might be a structured song. It may also be a song no one hears. It could be in a room in your work place that is empty but needs a change in the atmosphere. Sing it out and then observe what happens and what you can learn from the experience. Write them in your journal.

Chapter Four

HOW TO RELEASE HEAVEN'S SONG:
Singing What You See

In this section I want to give you some practical exercises and examples that can help develop heaven's song in you. These ideas are taken from my experience in both writing and singing, but also releasing songs to the public.

Singing what you see

Singing what you see could be something you see with your spirit eyes or an open vision. It can also include hearing the voice of God, whether audibly or spiritually.

This is a very powerful tool that can build as you increase in your prophetic gifting. Singing out what you see in your spirit is a great way to change the atmosphere. This is because when you verbally declare what you sense and see, you are partnering and agreeing with what is happening in the spiritual realm.

2 Corinthians 4:18 NIV
"So we fix our eyes not on what is seen but on what is unseen. For what is seen is temporary but what is unseen is eternal."

When you sing out from the unseen, you are tapping into what is eternal. You are pulling eternity into the present. You are drawing from something bigger than what is around you.

I love how *The Message* translation puts it:

2 Corinthians 4:18 MSG
"There's far more here than meets the eye. The things we see now are here today, gone tomorrow. But the things we can't see now will last forever."

If the things that we can't see now last forever, we should be singing about what we don't see. We are tapping in to something eternal as opposed to singing/writing songs about temporal things that are "here today, gone tomorrow."

There have been times when I have been leading worship when I have sensed something happening in the spirit realm that needed to be released into the atmosphere. I remember singing a song about the death and resurrection of Jesus Christ when in a moment I had a deep revelation of how powerful it was that Christ had risen. I know we know this and are grateful for it, but I love the moment when it hits your spirit and it becomes revelation to you all over again in a greater measure than before. I felt so overwhelmed by the fact that our God is risen! Immediately thoughts began running around in my head: *"Yes, there are other gods in the earth that battle for authority. Yes, there are many spiritual forces trying to prove their power. But Jesus is the only God that has risen from the dead. He is the only God that has taken the keys of hell and death. If the same power that raised Christ from the dead lives in me, then I have more authority than I have imagined!"*

I became so moved by this thought. I also understood that it was something the Lord was trying to reveal to me. If it was released in the atmosphere it would bring revelation to others. In that moment I also understood that when believers take hold of that revelation and understand that "greater is He that is in me than he that is in the world," (1 John 4:4) we become overcomers in any situation.

So I began to sing out phrases prophetically: *"Death where is your sting? My God is alive! Nothing could hold Him in the grave!"* I immediately felt a "snap" in the atmosphere – a change that happened so quickly. The congregation roared and clapped as they too began to engage and agree with what was being sung. It will go down in my memory as one of my most favorite corporate worship experiences – when every single person in the room was engaged and electrified by the power of God.

Another time was when I wrote "Footsteps of my Father." I was leading worship at a prayer meeting when all of the sudden I saw in my spirit the Lord beginning to walk through the congregation and touch people on their shoulders. I could see Him walking through the room looking into the hearts of the people to see what their needs were. So I began to play a musical interlude on the piano that sounded like footsteps. Then I began to sing, *"I can hear the footsteps of my father, I can hear the footsteps of my God, walking through the hallways of my heart."*

Singing out what you see reveals to others what the Lord is doing. This can help people receive in greater measure.

Personal revelation verses corporate revelation

One thing we need to be mindful of when we sing out what we see is if what we are experiencing is a personal revelation – something the Lord is trying to teach *you*, or if it is a corporate revelation – something He is trying to reveal to His *church*.

I have heard a lot of prophetic songs that were very personal in a corporate setting but it actually became distracting, because it was a word for the person who was singing it – not for the congregation. Sometimes of course, they are one and the same but it is only by growing in wisdom that we understand when we are meant to release what we see in a song, or if it's God wanting to reveal something to us.

Some questions to ask yourself in that moment are:

1. Lord, is this a revelation for me, or for everyone?

2. Am I the person to sing this out, or am I just sensing something that is in the atmosphere? This is *very* important, because often when you increase in your prophetic gifting you will be sensing a lot of things just because you are prophetic. It doesn't always mean it is

meant to be released verbally or musically. It's just you being aware of what is happening.

If you don't understand what you are seeing
This has happened to me lots of times. I will not sing something out if I don't have an understanding of what I am seeing. This is because I don't want to add confusion or bring tension into an atmosphere.

However, sometimes the Lord will reveal to me an understanding of a portion of a vision or idea. I have noticed He often does this because He wants to partner with me and He wants me to trust Him. It is a wonderful thought that the Lord will use you and be teaching you at the same time!

So I will often begin to sing just what I know. Often when I do this, as I am singing, more of the revelation is released to me. Sometimes it just takes that step of faith to step out and then you and the Lord move together. It's scary but also wonderful! It definitely makes you realize you are not in charge, God is!

Be encouraged that you can do this! It is not for a select few. It takes faith. Be confident in the unseen.

Hebrews 11:1 (The Message)
"The fundamental fact of existence is that this trust in God, this faith, is the firm foundation under everything that makes life worth living. It's our handle on what we can't see."

Singing into the atmosphere, not about the atmosphere

We sing *into* an atmosphere, not *about* the atmosphere. For example, you may be worship leading in a corporate setting and notice people are not engaging or people are apathetic. You might have a strong sense that a spirit of depression is in the room. When this happens, it is important that our song is not about that spirit. The way to bring release and breakthrough is to sing the answer.

If I was in a situation where I sensed this, I would sing words like *"a spirit of freedom has entered the room,"* or *"we turn our eyes to you"* or *"light a fire within us."* I prefer to partner with what God wants to do rather than what is happening.

I love what Graham Cooke says: "fight in the opposite spirit." This is a powerful tool when releasing heaven's song.

SUMMARY – Singing What You See

1. You can sing a spontaneous song or craft a song from a vision or something you are sensing in the moment.

2. We need to learn to sense whether it is a personal word (for you) or a corporate word (for others around you).

3. Sometimes you may only have a portion of a prophetic song but as you begin to sing it out, you receive more. So step out in faith!

4. Sing into the atmosphere, not about the atmosphere. Fight in the opposite spirit!

ACTIONS

1. Is there a time you can remember where you have seen something in the spirit, or heard God's voice (audibly or His still small voice)? What did it feel like? Did you share it with the congregation, or speak it out at home in your personal worship time? What happened when you did this? If you are in a small group setting share some stories, or write in your personal journal.

2. Right now ask the Lord to show you something. Don't have an agenda. Just allow Him to speak to you about anything. What is He saying? As you hear Him speak, experiment with singing it out. It could be a few phrases, or one word. Just sing what is comfortable. What does it feel like to express this? Discuss with the group or write in your journal your experience.

3. If the image was particularly powerful, try writing a crafted song around the theme.

Chapter Five

HOW TO RELEASE HEAVEN'S SONG:
Singing What You Dream

Singing what you have dreamed

I am talking about a literal dream that you have had when you are sleeping but I am also including dreams and visions you may have had while you were awake. This could be an open vision – where you have seen something with your physical eyes or a dream you have had whilst sleeping.

In the scriptures the Lord often spoke in dreams, or "night visions," so we can be confident today that this is one way the Lord can speak to us:

Job 33:14-15 NIV
"For God does speak – now one way, now another – though man may not perceive it. In a dream, in a vision of the night, when deep sleep falls on men as they slumber in their beds..."

Genesis 46:2 NIV

"*And God spoke to Israel in a vision at night and said, 'Jacob! Jacob!' 'Here I am,' he replied.*"

Dreams can reveal mysteries or bring things to your understanding:

Daniel 2:19 NIV

"*During the night the mystery was revealed to Daniel in a vision. Then Daniel praised the God of heaven.*"

Dreams can reveal what is happening in the spiritual realm that is impacting the physical realm:

Zachariah 1:8 NIV

"*During the night I had a vision – and there before me was a man riding a red horse! He was standing among the myrtle trees in a ravine. Behind him were red, brown and white horses.*"

Dreams can reveal the "next step":

Acts 16:9 NIV

"*During the night Paul had a vision of a man of Macedonia standing and begging him, 'Come over to Macedonia and help us.'*"

Dreams can bring encouragement:

Acts 18:9 NIV
"One night the Lord spoke to Paul in a vision: 'Don't be afraid; keep on speaking, don't be silent...'"

The Lord often speaks to me in dreams. I think this is because He can't get a word in during the day! Often dreams are revealed to us so that we can understand what is going on "behind the scenes," or God is showing us something that is about to happen. This often brings me peace and shows me what to pray, but also what to write or sing. Sometimes a dream is given to us by God so that we are made aware of something. It is drawing our focus to a particular theme.

It could be a dream about the nations, or it could be something personal that reveals an attribute of God. Sometimes He may reveal it to you a few days before you are to lead worship in a corporate setting or it could also be something He wants you to sing in your personal worship time at home (this is especially true if it's more of a personal revelation about something happening to you personally).

Some things that have helped me develop in this are:

1. Have a dream book or a file on your computer where you can write down the date, time and content of your dream. If you understand the interpretation, write that down as well.

2. If you don't understand the interpretation, is there someone you can dialogue with that can help you interpret the dream?

3. Often a dream will contain a theme or an element that is important. When writing or singing this, don't feel you have to include the "story" of the dream. It is more important to have the theme come out. For example, the dream could be about revival in your city. Write down some words that remind you of what the dream is about. Include this language in your singing/songwriting. Also don't feel you have to include everything. Sometimes it is only part of the dream the Lord wants revealed, yet He includes more for you to see so you have context.

4. Sometimes it helps to sit on it a while. As you ponder the dream more will be revealed to you. Take the time

for it to brew in you, unless you have a sense it is something you have to release sooner.

5. Obviously not all dreams are for corporate revelation. Is the dream you received for you personally, or is it something that needs to be shared? Sometimes it can also be both – what God is revealing personally to you is something He also wants to reveal to His church.

SUMMARY – Singing What You Dream

1. You can sing a prophetic song inspired by a dream or a vision.

2. There is evidence throughout scripture the God speaks through dreams and visions.

3. Dreams contain themes of what the Lord wants to reveal to you.

ACTIONS

1. Think of a dream you have had that left an impact on you that you believe was given to you by the Lord. Write down the dream down in your journal, or discuss in your group. What was the general theme of the dream? How did it impact you? What do you think the Lord was trying to say to you?

2. Practice singing out the general theme. Remember that you don't need to tell the story; it's more about what the Lord is trying to say. Also remember, keep it simple and if something is important, repeat it.

3. Sing out spontaneously what God was trying to say to you in a worship team rehearsal workshop on this topic. Sing a song out, and then discuss what people saw when you sang out. Did you get the message across? What did people feel when you sang it? This can be quite daunting but also a great way to increase in confidence and skill. Remember you don't need to tell a story; it's all about themes! Let others experiment with this idea as well. We often learn by watching how others release the song of the Lord.

4. Does your dream align itself with scripture? Write down three or four verses that resonate with the dream you have had.

Chapter Six

HOW TO RELEASE HEAVEN'S SONG:
Singing Prophetic Words

Singing from a prophetic word

I believe that music has a way of softening people. You can put prophetic words to melody and song and it is received in a way that possibly may not be received if it was just spoken.

What is also powerful about writing songs from prophetic words is that it becomes memorable as it is something that people can sing along to. Then it means more people are partnering with what God is saying. People are coming into agreement with what has been spoken out.

A few years ago our church put together a prayer that carried the vision of where we felt we were headed. It was written from a prophetic word from our senior leaders. One day in church as we were reading it from the screen as a congregation, the Lord spoke to me and said, *"You need to write a song with those themes."* I had never even thought of this idea before but it burned so strongly in me that I began to explore the idea.

I pulled out key words that caught my attention. I pulled out key themes that I felt were important for our church in that season. From that prophetic word, I wrote a song called "More of You." It was a simple song but it was such a joy to see the congregation pick it up and sing it with all their hearts every Sunday for many months. It was wonderful to be a part of helping people engage with the prophetic word for our church.

I am going to show you the prophetic word below, then show you the lyrics that I wrote, so you can see an example of how to release heaven's song via a prophetic word:

Crafted Prayer

Father we declare Your majesty and Your sovereignty as we enter into this year of training and of proclaiming Your favor.

We thank you Lord that You have adopted us as a community of faith to release heaven here on Earth. We ask Lord for Your grace and empowering as we dig a well of favor for others to draw from.

We come into agreement with You Lord as we choose to put aside doubt and passivity to be the people You have called us to be:
A people with an incredible mindset about You; a people full of vision of who You are; a people passionate for You; a people free from every bondage; a people free to be extraordinary in You.

We thank You for this opportunity to learn to believe like we have never believed before; to overcome; to confess and stand on Your word so that situations fall to us; to rise up; to persist; to defy the enemy; to embrace Your favor; to experience sensational joy; to be outrageous; to breakthrough; to be an ordinary people having extraordinary encounters with You.

Lord we choose to align our thoughts, words and actions with our identity and heritage as Your sons and daughters.

We thank You that we are able to give away, for Your glory and honor, the favor that You pour into our lives.

Amen.

And now the song...

MORE OF YOU
Words and music: Roma Waterman

Lord we declare your majesty
Above all else it's you we seek
With passion we rise to follow you
Your purpose in everything we do

Our heart's cry is to know you more
To live beneath the shadow of your wings

More of your power
More of your Glory
More of your Love Mighty King
Pour your anointing
Over your people
We're falling in love with you

Lord we want more of You
We want more of you

As your mighty army we will rise
For souls of the lost we stand and fight
Leading them to your mercy seat
Moving in time to your heartbeat

Your people adore you
We bow down before you
We're falling in love with you more everyday
We lift up our praises
Our hearts with Thanksgiving
To bring you the glory that's due to your name

As you can see, I didn't always use exact phrasing. Sometimes this is possible and if you feel led to include things word for word, yet can craft your song in a way that is easy to sing – then go for it!

What happens when you sing/write from a prophetic word

You release God's atmosphere over and over again. You are calling what is not as though it is. As you do this, you redeem what is in the future into the present. As you declare His words, even though you may feel or see something different presently that what is being spoken, you pull His reality into the current reality.

You are also helping others grasp God's words by providing a simple and memorable format that helps them repeat what He has promised.

There is also something powerful about a community of people singing the same word. As a community of believers join together in unity to declare the promise from God, we create a strong bond not only with the heavenly realm but with each other.

A spontaneous song from a prophetic word
You can also use this model if you want to sing spontaneously, rather than crafting a structured song. For example, you may be leading worship, or spending time at home in your prayer time and a prophetic word comes to mind. If a specific theme or word stands out, sing it out! It doesn't have to be long (sometimes it's more productive if it isn't) – it could be a few words.

"Song Prayers"

You can also add a "song prayer" to a prophetic word. For example, if a word given was something like, "You will release the sound of heaven over this nation," you could add a prayer by singing, "Release your song within us Lord. Let it pour out over our nation." This is powerful because sometimes there may be hindrances to that prophetic word coming to pass. Your "song prayer" can help release a stronghold, or bring revelation that brings a breakthrough.

SUMMARY – Singing Prophetic Words

1. You can take prophetic words and turn them into prophetic songs.

2. This helps us partner with what God is saying.

3. It helps people remember God's prophetic word.

4. It creates unity amongst a community of believers.

5. You can sing a spontaneous song or write a structured song from a prophetic word.

6. You can release "song prayers" in agreement to a prophetic word.

ACTIONS

1. Take a prophetic word that is either a corporate word for your people group, church or a word you have received personally. Write down key words/phrases that stand out to you. Don't write out whole sections but rather find words or short phrases that stand out to you.

2. Now add some visions that you see to your "brainstorming" page. What do you see/understand when you read these words? For example, when I saw the words "Lord we declare Your majesty," I thought of the Lord on His throne, in power and in strength. Write these down.

3. From your brainstorming page, try and write a song. Keep in mind for it to be memorable it needs to be simple with not too many lyrics. It also helps if there are repetitive sections both in the melody and the lyrics so that it can be easy to sing along to.

4. Don't feel you have to include everything in your song – just what stands out to you. What stands out often is what the Holy Spirit wants to highlight.

5. Another good idea is to keep a record book of all the prophetic words that are important to you. Regularly get them out and read them. Has anything changed? Has anything not come to pass? If so, turn it into a song and continue to speak out God's truths. When you do this, you have strategy. You have a plan. Don't wait for those prophetic words to come to you – run out and grab them!

6. As a worship team, or in your personal time, take out some prophetic words that mean something to you. Spontaneously sing out certain lines. Add a "song prayer" to these prophetic words to affirm you come into agreement with what God is saying. Do you need to sing anything out to release breakthrough and break down strongholds?

Chapter Seven

HOW TO RELEASE HEAVEN'S SONG:
Singing Scripture

It can be quite daunting to sing something that is the overflow of your heart and that is why singing the scriptures is a great way to delve into the prophetic song. In fact it is one of the easiest ways if you are just starting out. That is not to say that it is only a starting point and after you become more experienced you no longer need it – quite the opposite. Scripture is always going to be good because it is the word of God. When we sing out His words, we are agreeing with them. It's always going to be accurate!

Singing scripture is also a great tool in starting a prophetic worship time in your personal time with God, or if the culture of your church is more of the spontaneous song, starting a service using scripture is a great introduction.

The important thing again is making sure there is not too much content. Just take a verse or two and sing them over and over.

Some questions to ask yourself as you are doing this are:

1. Is there one theme, or phrase that needs to be sung over and over? Choose what you feel needs emphasis.

2. Is this a song I want the congregation to sing, or one I just want to sing out? If it's one for the congregation it needs to be simple and easy to learn. That way people will feel comfortable to join in. If it's to sing out, then you can take more liberties with melody and words, it can be longer, it can have different sections, etc.

Experiment using different Bible translations. It's a great way to study the word and understand what you are singing. When at home in my personal time, I love using the *Message* translation, as it's so visual and creative.

Find a scripture that has meaning to you – that's often God's way of highlighting what it is He wants you to sing. Often when something is familiar or comfortable to us, or we are drawn to something, we can often think it's not important because it's too easy or obvious. We often don't realize it is so obvious because that is what God wants to say or express.

Let me show you an example of how I used scripture to form a song during my own personal worship time.

Proverbs 3:5-6 NIV
"Trust in the Lord with all of your heart and lean not on your own understanding; in all your ways acknowledge him and he will make your paths straight."

From that, I wrote a simple song:

I trust in the Lord with all of my heart
I don't depend on my own understanding
I trust in the Lord with all of my heart
And He will direct my paths

Lord I trust you, my life's in your hands
Surrendering all to your mighty plan
Lord I trust you with all that I am
And you will direct my paths.

It is pretty simple but at the time I sang it out, I really needed it to become a revelation in my spirit.

I find one simple rule to go by is to go with the very first thought that emerges in my mind when I begin to search for heaven's song.

If a scripture "lights up" in your mind, go with it. Even if it feels strange at first, I try to be bold and step out. One thing my friend Dan McCollam often says which has helped me a lot is instead of asking *"Is this just me?"* ask *"Is that you God?"* It changes the whole dynamic of how you think. It allows you to put more trust in your ability to hear from God, rather than your ability to mess up!

Philippians 1:6 MSG
"There has never been the slightest doubt in my mind that the God who started this great work in you would keep at it and bring it to a flourishing finish on the very day Christ Jesus appears."

He started something good in you and He will finish it. Trust that you are hearing from God and step into all He has called you to be instead of allowing the spirit of intimidation and doubt to cloud your judgment. God speaks to ordinary people just like you and me.

SUMMARY – Singing Scripture

1. Singing scripture is a good starting point when you are learning how to delve into the prophetic song.

2. When we sing scripture we are agreeing and speaking out God's words.

3. Keep it simple and concise.

4. Be more confident in your ability to hear from God rather than allowing intimidation to stop you from singing the prophetic song.

ACTION

As a worship team:

1. Choose a Psalm that glorifies/worships God. As the band plays a simple chord progression (2-4 chords in 4/4 is a good start) choose 4-5 singers to stand in line. Allow each singer to sing a portion of the scripture. It could be a verse, it could be three of four words;

2. Each singer should repeat phrases or words that stand out to them. Each person should have around 2 minutes each (don't drag it out). As one person finishes, allow the next person to sing the next portion of scripture. As this is happening, the rest of the worship team should be listening so that there can be general discussion later.

3. After about 10 minutes, discuss together what each singer experienced as they sang out. Some questions to ask are "Why did you feel to repeat that phrase?" "What did you 'see' in your spirit as you sang this out?"

4. Something else that can be effective is to have a back line of singers (if you have a lot of singers, if not, use who you have!) repeating phrases as the main singer is

releasing them. If something stands out to you, sing it over and over as a refrain that others can sing along to. Encourage the singers to pick up on this and be bold and sing along. This also helps the whole worship team remain engaged as they become more aware that their involvement is integral in releasing heaven's song in a corporate setting.

5. It is a great idea to record these times so that you can listen to it again. If you have the equipment, just hit record and keep it running.

In your personal worship time:

1. You can do the above on your own and adapt it to suit your setting and needs.

2. Choose a few translations of the Bible to sing your scripture out. It's a great way to gain more insight into a verse or chapter.

3. If you normally play an instrument, use it to enhance your use of singing the scriptures. However, another idea is to either move to another instrument that you are not as fluent on to accompany yourself on. When

we use the same forum to write and sing we can often become desensitized or not pay attention – we are so used to doing things a certain way that we do not approach things with a fresh and unique mindset. If you are a piano player for example, yet know two or three chords on the guitar, switch to guitar for a few minutes to sing out the scripture. You will often move to a different chord progression on a different instrument. This changes the melody and intention of a scripture. You may even notice you sing things differently or different words stand out to you when you do this.

4. If you don't play an instrument, just sing a melody line to your scripture. You don't have to be an incredible musician to sing the song of the Lord. You have the song of the Lord in you whether you are musical or not! You just need to be hungry.

5. If you don't feel it is working, here are some tips:

    a) Change the key you are singing in – often singing too high means you have nowhere to move to melodically as you progress into a song or singing too low makes it hard for you to connect your voice with the lyrics.

    b) Change the scripture! We don't always get it right straight away. It can take time to really reach the heart of what God is trying to emphasize.

    c) Change Bible translations.

6. When you finish your quiet time singing the song of the Lord using scripture, journal your experience. What was it like? Did some good song ideas come out of the session? What do you feel the Lord was trying to emphasize? Was it for a personal revelation or a corporate revelation for a later time in a church setting? Is it something that can be crafted into a structured song/congregational song? As you were singing, what did you see?

Chapter Eight

HOW TO RELEASE HEAVEN'S SONG:
Singing What You Feel

You may have grown up in an era where emotions were frowned upon in the church or in society and taught that to be led by our emotions is wrong. This is partly true and partly untrue. I want to preface this chapter with saying that being an emotion-driven person is not what I am talking about here. We always want to be led by the Spirit in all we do and also aligning what we sing, speak and live by with the scriptures – not how we are feeling at any given time.

Sometimes aligning ourselves with what the Lord wants us to do can go against the emotional response we are feeling. I have to be honest and say there have been many times when the Lord has asked me to do things and I have initially not wanted to do them! My emotional response was that I did not want to be embarrassed, make a mistake or even be vulnerable. I like to think I obey the Lord when He asks me to do things that go against how I am feeling. Emotions can be deceptive and do not always tell the story of what is really going on.

However, it does not mean that our emotions are evil or that we should not have an emotional response to things. There have been just as many times that I have not enjoyed my emotional response to things and there are also just as many times that I have felt great emotion and it has been appropriate. Emotion and a renewed mind coupled with wisdom and an understanding of the scriptures makes a very powerful combination.

Reference to emotions in the scriptures

There are many times in the Bible where people released a song or an outburst of praise that was directly related to their emotions.

King David

David danced naked before the Lord with all his might:

2 Samuel 6:14
"David, wearing a linen ephod, danced before the LORD with all his might,"

I like what the below commentary states:

> ***David danced before the Lord*** *– The Hebrews, like other ancient people, had their sacred dances, which were performed on their solemn anniversaries and other great occasions of commemorating some special token of the divine goodness and favor.*
>
> ***With all his might*** *– intimating violent efforts of leaping and divested of his royal mantle (in a state of undress), conduct apparently unsuitable to the gravity of age or the dignity of a king. But it was unquestionably done as an act of religious homage, his attitudes and dress being symbolic, as they have always been in Oriental countries, of penitence, joy, thankfulness and devotion."* [7]

I can imagine David was so caught up in joy and thanksgiving, he did not care that he was the King or how he appeared to others.

Moses and Miriam

Moses and Miriam sang a spontaneous song the next morning after crossing the Red Sea. The scripture says that

---

[7] *Commentary Critical and Explanatory on the Whole Bible.*

the Israelites also joined in song – that's an estimated 3 million people!

Exodus 15:1 NIV
"Then Moses and the Israelites sang this song to the LORD: "I will sing to the LORD, for he is highly exalted. The horse and its rider he has hurled into the sea."

Exodus 15:21 NIV
"Miriam sang to them: "Sing to the LORD, for He is highly exalted. The horse and its rider he has hurled into the sea."

Again, I love this explanation from the *Critical and Explanatory Commentary*:

> **"I will sing unto the Lord, for he hath triumphed gloriously**–Considering the state of servitude in which they had been born and bred and the rude features of character which their subsequent history often displays, it cannot be supposed that the children of Israel generally were qualified to commit to memory or to appreciate the beauties of this inimitable song. But they might perfectly understand its pervading strain of sentiment; and with the view of suitably improving the occasion, it was thought necessary that all, old and

young, should join their united voices in the rehearsal of its words. As every individual had cause, so every individual gave utterance to his feelings of gratitude."[8]

I don't know about you but the last thing on my mind straight after being chased by an army ready to kill me would be to write a song. When emotion is involved however, there is an overflow of the heart that happens that cannot be contained. As a side note, I also love how this commentary intimates that the song was most likely being sung in their own way – that many people trying to sing something in unison, coupled with them learning how it was to be sung is an interesting combination! I wonder if it was much like a free worship time in a service, where everyone was singing the same theme, yet singing it in their own different way – partnering with what they were hearing around them and then translating it in their own unique way – all at the same time!

Moses, Miriam and the Israelites just experienced God move in an incredibly powerful way. A whole sea parting to set a people free and the destruction of the Egyptian army was such a declaration of God to His people that He was for

---

[8] *Commentary Critical and Explanatory on the Whole Bible.*

them. Can you imagine the uproar when they got to the other side?

I wonder if it was a simple melody that the Israelites could hear as it echoed down through the camp. It has been said there were over three million Israelites who escaped from Egypt. Can you imagine Moses and Miriam releasing that song when there were no microphones or MP3's that could be scattered through the crowds of people – yet it translated in such a way and had so much impact that it was recorded in Exodus for every generation afterward to see. Theologians say that this is one of the oldest and most eloquent poems by some few hundred years recorded in history. A song rising from all of them as they begin to echo the praises of God.

Joshua and the Battle of Jericho

In Joshua chapter six we have the story recorded of The Battle of Jericho. After they had marched around the walls of Jericho seven times, a shout was released on the seventh day. I can't imagine they were bored or did it with a sigh in their hearts. Imagine the anticipation! They were full of excitement, declaration and battle cries, that when the sound was released, it came from the pit of their bellies and roared through their stomachs until it catapulted out of their mouths.

Experiencing God through your five senses

Your five senses are important. Sometimes the Lord will also use them to reveal something to you. Much like we know a baby is coming when labor pains are experienced and we can also experience the beginnings of what the Lord is wanting to release. Below are some examples.

Flesh

It is not just our hearts that longs for God but also our flesh:

Psalm 16:9 KJV
"Therefore my heart is glad and my glory rejoiceth:
my flesh also shall rest in hope."

Psalm 84:2 KJV
"My soul yearns, even faints, for the courts of the LORD;
my heart and my flesh cry out for the living God."

Even Jesus became emotional when He saw Mary and her friends weeping over the death of Lazarus:

> *John 11:33 KJV*
> *"When Jesus therefore saw her weeping and the Jews also weeping which came with her, he groaned in the spirit and was troubled."*

Let's read what this commentary suggests:

> **"When Jesus . . . saw her weeping and the Jews . . . weeping . . . he groaned in the spirit** – *the tears of Mary and her friends acting sympathetically upon Jesus and drawing forth His emotions. What a vivid and beautiful out coming of His 'real' humanity! The word here rendered 'groaned' does not mean 'sighed' or 'grieved,' but rather 'powerfully checked His emotion' – made a visible effort to restrain those tears which were ready to gush from His eyes.*
> **and was troubled** *– rather, 'troubled himself' (Margin); referring probably to this visible difficulty of repressing His emotions."*[9]

---
[9] *Commentary Critical and Explanatory on the Whole Bible.*

Taste

Psalm 34:8 NIV
"Taste and see that the LORD is good; blessed is the man who takes refuge in him."

Psalm 119:103 NIV
"How sweet are your words to my taste, sweeter than honey to my mouth!"

I am aware that these scriptures may not be literal but the point I am trying to convey is that these verses are comparing the sweetness of God to a taste experience! It is describing a spiritual attribute by using the physical sense of taste.

When David wrote "your words are sweeter than honey to my mouth," he was explaining that the taste of honey as beautiful as it is, is not as sweet as the words from God. So in essence, he is using his taste senses to remind him of an attribute of God. This is using your five senses in action.

Smell

Another example of this comparison is when Jesus received the woman who broke the expensive alabaster box and poured perfume over his head and feet (Mark 14). Imagine that scene for a moment. In the Eastern heat and sweaty dust, as she poured out this expensive oil, their vapors a striking contrast – imminently reviving and refreshing. It would have been so strong and almost overpowering. I remember someone bringing me back a gift of anointing oil from Jerusalem. Just opening the bottle would fill the house with such a strong smell. Imagine what it must have been like to pour a whole bottle out! What did it represent? It was a spiritual act that was emphasized by a physical sense of smell.

Allowing how we feel to be led by the Holy Spirit

Please understand that I am not saying we should be led by our emotions. Our spirit, soul, and body work together best when the Holy Spirit leads. This means our spirit is always activated by the Holy Spirit. He is not leading part of us, He is leading *all* of us, spirit, soul and body. However, what I am saying is that because of this Holy Spirit leading, it is not just our spirit being made alert to His voice but also our soul and body. If we are attentive to that, we will be able to tap into what the Lord is trying to say through our physical and emotional responses to things.

For example, someone was telling me recently that they sat down to watch a movie and it was expressing so much evil and fear that they became physically sick and had to stop watching it. This is a physical manifestation to a spiritual atmosphere. I can recall a time when I was in someone's house and a person walked in the door and before I even knew who they were, the moment they set foot in the door, I felt physically ill. I knew immediately the Lord was trying to warn me about this person. Later on my instincts were proved correct. My spirit was being made alert to a spiritual condition and it caused my physical senses to react.

The Lord does not always use the ear gate to speak. You may feel something (a burning in your hands, etc.), you may taste something, or see something. Instead of dismissing it as something unexplainable, allow your physical senses to be used by God. Led by the Holy Spirit's leading, you will hear God more than you could have ever imagined.

God is speaking – are we listening?
So many people say to me, *"I never hear God speak to me."* I want to encourage you – He is speaking more than you think. He is speaking in more than just a voice or words on a page. If He can speak through a donkey, surely we can expand our minds to understand that God can use anything and everything! He didn't just create your spirit, He created

all of you. So He will engage all of you – body, soul, and spirit when He wants to communicate with you.

So how do we recognize His voice through physical manifestations? Firstly, just being aware and open will activate this. In fact, some of you may be realizing as you read this that He has been speaking to you all along and you have not recognized it. Here are some examples I have experienced and other people I know have experienced that may help broaden your understanding:

- Some people experience heat in their hands and understand this means there is a healing anointing present. They know this means they can lay hands on people and they will see the Lord manifest His healing power.

- I have often smelled different fragrances in the room during personal worship times and corporate gatherings. I immediately know that this means the presence of the Lord is very real and present. Of course we know that the Lord is always with us but smelling a fragrance acts as a reminder that He is there. It becomes very tangible. During those times I have become incredibly alert to the realness of who He is.

- Sometimes what the smell is often can have meaning also. During those times often different smells can also represent different things. For example, I know this can sound crazy but let's also remember that different fragrances in the Bible represented different things. Most scholars concur that the frankincense and myrrh that was presented to Jesus as a child had meaning. Frankincense, an aromatic gum from trees used in worship, healing, and priesthood; Myrrh a symbol of suffering, death, and new life. In the tabernacle of Moses we read in Revelation 5:8 that the bowls of incense represented the prayers of the saints.

- Some people can experience different pains/symptoms in parts of their body. This is often the Lord revealing that people in the room have certain conditions that need healing. For example, someone may feel a pain in their knees or joints. Upon asking the Lord why they feel that pain, they may sense the Lord saying it has to do with arthritis in the knees/joints. Upon speaking that out, they release faith into the atmosphere and that person experiencing that condition can be healed.

So how do we, in releasing heaven's song, sing what we feel? There are many times where it is appropriate to use melodies and words to express feelings and impressions. If you are leading worship or involved in a soaking or prayer time, singing into the atmosphere is more fitting and less intrusive than stopping to talk about things. Sometimes, it's even more powerful because it becomes part of the worship experience, as opposed to breaking up the flow to stop and speak.

The comment in the previous chapter about singing *into* the atmosphere, not *about* the atmosphere is relevant here. For practical application, I have put some examples below:

- If you felt pain in your knees or joints, you may want to sing out something like, "Healing is flowing right now. Healing is pouring into joints and bringing freedom," or "Arthritis must bow its knee to the healing power of Jesus."

- If you experienced the taste sensation of honey, as you explore this with the Lord and how the scriptures refer to honey, you may sing out "His love is sweeter the honey, His words are like honey to my lips."

- If you smelled a strong perfume, you may sing "Your presence fills the room like perfume," or "Let our praises be as incense rising up to You."

Please keep in mind that everything is subjective. Each experience depends on the person receiving the sensation and how they interpret it. Everyone's life experience will mean they process different things different ways. It is vital you remain connected to the Holy Spirit to pour out the correct interpretation.

SUMMARY – Singing What You Feel

1. Emotions are not wrong or sinful.

2. There are references to emotions in the scriptures.

3. God will use our five senses to speak to us about what is happening in the spiritual realm.

4. You can use this to sing and write songs to bring breakthrough.

ACTIONS

As a worship team:

1. Next time you and the team are leading worship, or during a worship rehearsal, be aware of what is happening on the inside of you. Start singing a structured song together that is on your heart. This is a good exercise to practice in a rehearsal as opposed to a service if you are learning. If you are not on the platform but in the congregation, you can also participate in this exercise. Firstly, are you feeling anything in your physical body that is unusual? *E.g.* a burning in your hands, a pain in your body that you would not normally experience. Ask the Lord what it represents. Does the burning mean there is a healing anointing present? Does that pain represent someone who needs healing in their body?

2. Is there a structured song that reflects this? Can you sing this? If not, what can you sing out/pray out in between songs, or in a spontaneous worship time that would reflect this? Sing it into the atmosphere. Heavens' song isn't always a spontaneous song. It can be a structured song that is right for that specific

moment. It could be a Psalm, an old hymn, or something that has recently been written. What does God want you to do?

3. Another option is to think of what scripture reference reflects how you are feeling. Try singing this, or pausing to read this. Try a "song prayer" – sing out that healing. Sing out the scripture that is impressed upon your heart. It could be "He is the Lord that heals us – He sends His word and heals our disease," as an example.

4. As an instrumentalist in the worship team, be intentional about your playing. If healing was a sound, what would it sound like? If freedom was a sound, what would it sound like? It is possible and powerful to play your instrument and minister, just like David did over Saul and for the atmosphere to be changed. David played peace with his harp over a troubled Saul and the evil spirits left him. What is the impression on your heart and how can you convey that with your instrument?

5. It is also powerful just to sing out a note. There have been many times when I have felt to sing something out

but not use words. Sometimes that sound is not lyrics – it can be a note or a few notes.

You may have seen film of opera singers singing so high that a wine glass shatters into pieces. This is because the frequency of the singer's note is matching the frequency of the wine glass. As they both resonate on the same frequency, it causes the glass to break. When you sing the sound that is right for the moment that is exactly what happens – you are releasing a sound that brings breakthrough in a situation. The key is finding that sound! You will only know if you try, while being sensitive to what the Holy Spirit is doing and what He is trying to show you.

6. Always try to make time to debrief, or discuss afterwards with the team. Always be encouraging but be honest. Sometimes we are going to miss it because we are human – don't be discouraged by this. The only way we will become more effective in what we do is to keep doing it. The more you step out, the more you will grow.

In your personal worship time:

7. Think of a specific attribute of God and who He is. Choose a song that reflects this. It says in the scriptures *"I will to enter His gates with thanksgiving in my heart, I will enter His courts with praise."* (Psalm 100:4) To enter into God's presence, it's always great to start your worship time in praise and thanksgiving. Sing for a few minutes and then if you feel led start to sing spontaneously or as your spirit leads.

8. After a while, begin to ask the Lord to show you things. He may bring up a particular situation. How do you feel when you think of this? What could you sing that would bring breakthrough or change the atmosphere? It could be one word, a short phrase, or even a sound. Experiment.

9. Think about a particular emotion you feel frequently that you don't like and you would like to see come under the influence of heaven. It could be anxiety, fear, anger, or depression. Think about what the opposite spirit of those feelings might be. Begin to sing over yourself in that opposite spirit. If it's fear, sing of peace. If it's depression, sing of joy and hope. Start

declaring over yourself those emotions you would like to see manifested in your life. It could be a spontaneous song from your own heart, or it could be a song that is already written that resonates with you. This is a great tool in releasing breakthrough in your own personal life.

Chapter Nine

Your Prophetic Identity as a Worshipper

Many worshippers underestimate the power and authority they can bring in their own sphere of influence. We can often make the mistake that because a song is well known, that song has more power than our own song. It is true that worship songs that have had an impact globally and nationally have a special mark on them and it's wonderful to see the body uniting to sing a song that resonates with a large group of people. However, your own song and you releasing that song is just as important, even if it does not reach the same amount of people.

If our reference point is to write songs that influence the secret place rather than the marketplace, then we should not allow how it is accepted in the marketplace to determine whether our song has influence or not.

Much like an intercessor enters their prayer closet and can pray for many years before an answer to prayer, we must also sing those songs whether others sing them, affirm them, or they provide financial gain. Don't let how others perceive your song to be the defining factor of you releasing it.

Have we allowed a performance spirit to enter in to our churches? We can easily become discouraged when our songs don't seem to have a voice in our congregations. This can cause songwriters and worship leaders to be silent. What is not being released that can only be released through you? I want to urge you to be silent no longer.

Understanding your identity as a worshipper is very important in helping you gain authority in this area. The main reason we don't release heaven's song is because we don't know who we are and we feel we don't have anything to bring. Once we have an understanding of our prophetic identity, we will have more understanding as to how, where, and what song should be released. This identity will be different for everyone and I hope in this chapter I can shed light on how to understand yourself a little more and how that relates to what you can bring. Most of this book contains ideas to give you strategy. But it is only effective if you have identity – if you know and are confident in who you are in Christ.

Where you authority lies

One reason why we don't see breakthrough with heaven's song is because we don't understand where our authority lies. It is possible that you may be trying to influence atmospheres in an area that you have no authority. Once you connect your song with the sphere that you have authority in, it is powerful. Knowing where you are meant to be and who you are meant to influence means you can "hit the target" rather than just anywhere on the dartboard!

When I began releasing radio singles, it became very clear that the demographic that was most impacted were women between the ages of 25-40 years old. Without intention in aiming at this age group, my songs were reaching them. For a season, when I was asked to speak and sing, it was often at women's events. If I had taken those songs and tried to sing them in an aged care facility, or in a kindergarten – I would probably be met with blank stares. *My authority was not in those areas.* Yet it was obvious that my influence was with this demographic.

When I began to sing prophetically and began leading worship, I was amazed at the effectiveness and peace I experienced. What seemed most natural to me, and therefore not requiring much effort, has had the greatest impact. Why? Because my calling is to release the prophetic and lead worship. It has taken me 20 years to realize this. This is the sphere of influence that I have grown into. When I connected my song to that, power from heaven was released in greater measure.

I also remember a time when I was first starting to sing I was asked to perform before a "life metal" band at a Christian festival. Who knows why the organizers thought that was a good combination, but I began my set performing to a crowd who was waiting for a very popular band to come on and perform. Most of the crowd were males in black heavy metal t-shirts and long hair! They were bored and they showed it! It was a terrible experience.

If I had taken that experience and put my identity in it, I would have made the assumption that what I have to offer has no influence or is not important. This is where many people end up in their thought process. They have an experience and because they did not *make* an impact, they think they *have* no impact. But it can often be because you are not ministering in what is *your* sphere of influence.

How to find your sphere of influence

This poses the question *"What is my sphere of influence?"* Another way of asking the question is *"What is my identity?"* Here are some thoughts I have:

1. **The thing that you love**

   Often what you are most drawn to is where your influence will lie (as long as it aligns with Kingdom thinking of course). As I look back on my own life, I see that I had always had a passion for worship. I ended up doing many things that did not fit into this paradigm and I found it difficult to have flow and traction. As soon as I began to lead worship I felt so at home. It was something that I loved but because it was so simple and I was naturally drawn to this form of expression, I did not realize it was actually what I was called to do.

   I am also drawn to connecting and uniting people. One of my favorite things to do is draw together worshippers from different denominations and to connect them to people they would not normally connect with. I love seeing the body of Christ come together, no matter what culture or church background they come from. I understand I have a sphere of influence in this area.

2. **Brings life to you and others**

    If you are really working in your gift, it should rejuvenate and bring life to you. I can spend all day recording in a studio or writing and although I may feel tired from a hard day's work, will feel full of life and energy. There have been times when I have done things, working in my gift, and hated it and felt exhausted. Why? Because I was using my gifts but using them in the wrong forum. I was not in my sphere of influence. I understand now I should be refueled and energized by what I am doing. It doesn't mean it won't be hard work, but it should be enjoyable.

3. **It is unique to you**

    One of the things I love about Kingdom living is that He calls us to different things that are unique to us. What He has called you to will be the right fit for you! It will be unique and fit right in with who you are, your likes and dislikes, your personality.

    We can spend much of our time trying to "fit the mold." We try to minister the way we think people would like to be ministered to. It's important to be sensitive to the needs of the demographic people group around us but it's just as important to be *you*. Be original.

There are people in our worship team who are brilliant at leading worship at corporate church services. Then there are others who are anointed worship leaders but their gift does not work in this paradigm. I have a friend who recently released an album singing worship songs over recorded sounds of nature and the forest. He is in his 50s and everything about what he does is unique. This album has fast become one of my favorites, because it is different. If he had tried to "fit the mold" his effectiveness would have been minimized. The anointing on what he does is amazing.

I have another friend who has an incredible gift of writing and producing plays at Christmas. She is a gifted singer and could have easily been a great worship leader. But when I go to her productions and I see what she has created, I am totally in awe. When she sings in these productions, I see her right where she is meant to be. These productions have an impact on so many people.

I could not do what these people do – it is unique to them. Be you.

4. It is bigger than you

If you feel what God has called you to is bigger than your resources and gifts, then you are most likely walking in your calling. I would even go as far to say if it's not bigger than you it's probably not God. In my 20+ years of being in the ministry, there has not been one season in my life that didn't require steps of faith and the confidence that I was really doing what God was asking me to do. It has seemed surreal at times, overwhelming, even impossible. There has never been the money in the bank to accomplish a task when I started – but it was always there when I needed it.

There have been many times when I have felt I didn't have what it takes to expand and create but I became that person during the process of stepping out. I have learned to understand that it's always going to be bigger than me and my resources. This is because God is also interested in your personal development and not just what you can bring. He wants to do something in you as His anointing pours out of you. He wants to give to you as you give to others. You don't get left out of being blessed yourself!

Don't just do what you know you can do. Do what you know God can do through you. *Dream.*

5. **It carries your testimony**

What you are called to will carry your story. You may not even realize this is happening as you step out. The overflow of our heart comes because of all Jesus has done for us. This pours out into everything we do. It also carries us in difficult times.

Many years ago I wanted to write a song for a girl in our youth group whose father had recently and unexpectedly committed suicide. My heart just ached for her. I was going to be singing at their youth service, so I asked the Lord to give me a song for her. I will never forget how easy and quickly the song "I Was Carried" came to me. As I completed the song I began to rehearse it alone in my home. I was brought to tears, because I realized this song was not just about her – it carried my testimony. It was my story – being carried in the arms of a stronger man in difficult times. I didn't know it then but that song has become the hearts cry for many people around the world because of the same reason. I did not expect this and have been so amazed at the stories I hear from people who the Lord has spoken to through it. I believe the song has had so much impact because it carries my testimony. It's my story.

Your testimony overcomes:

> *Revelation 12:11 NIV*
> *"They overcame him by the blood of the Lamb and by the word of their testimony; they did not love their lives so much as to shrink from death."*

The other side of this thought is that you can only release what has been released in you. Your testimony – how you met Jesus and how He has saved you, will spill out in to all that you do. Let it pour out.

For some, it manifests itself in the revelation you have personally received as you walk with God. For example, for me, I know God is good and He will provide for me. My identity always comes out of this because this is the revelation I have about the Lord. For others it could be peace, fulfillment, power, rest, or supernatural encounter. These are things we can experience as we walk with Him but your testimony will spotlight attributes of God because He ministers to us all in different ways, according to our situation and personality.

Working on your character

As we step into who we are in Christ, it may mean breaking bad habits and developing better ones. Working on our character is important in growing in our identity. This is because we can often be a certain way because of past hurts and disappointments and this can affect how we perceive and impart the prophetic message the Lord wants to reveal to us.

Maybe it comes out in how we deal with people or how we see ourselves, what we draw our confidence from, or how we work in our gifts. I want to be the best minister possible, so I am always looking at what needs growth in an area of my life. It doesn't mean it's comfortable or easy (or I even like working on it for that matter) but being aware of what needs to change in us can really help us have our confidence in who we are in Christ.

People that have an anointing will always release something special. This is an interesting conundrum because there are many people who have character issues that still can release something powerful, because of the gift that is on their life. The Lord will never take away what He has freely given us which is a wonderful attribute of God – that He would give us talents, abilities and anointing just because He chooses too, not because we have been well behaved or not. Thank goodness for that! However, there is something to be said about the Holiness of God and out of our respect for His holiness, wanting to change to be more like Him, because this is what He asks but it is also what He loves.

I feel quite sad when I see people moving so powerfully in their gift, yet not working on their inner life, or working on issues that may prevent them from growing in their anointing. For example, I have met many people in ministry who have such powerful influence, yet they treat people so badly.

A simple thing like spending more time in the secret place than on a platform, or learning to love and honor people is so pleasing to God. Some people are happy with where their gift goes as it's easy to go there. But there is always more. Why would we want to rely on the gift God so unreservedly gives us to move when we could also be completely connected to an ongoing flow that only comes out of relationship with Him? There is so much more than just being gifted.

There is treasure we have in our bank account (God gives a measure freely), but then there is the treasury of heaven. I can spend what I have from my treasure chest but eventually this will run out. It doesn't mean the anointing will leave me (*"For the gifts and callings of God are without repentance"* Romans 11:29) but I would rather delve into the treasury of heaven that is always plentiful and always abundant than just rely on what is in my hands.

This means addressing issues in my life that can cause a hindrance to this flow.

Talent and gifting may get you to where you want to go but character determines how long you will stay there.

Summary – Your Prophetic Identity as a Worshipper

1. When you understand where your authority lies, you will have greater impact in your sphere of influence.

2. Your identity:
   - is the thing that you love.
   - brings life to you and others.
   - is unique to you.
   - is bigger than you.
   - carries your testimony.

3. Working on your character helps release what is in you in greater measure.

ACTIONS

In your journal, or in a group discussion, write or discuss the following:

1. Think about your life right now – what things bring you energy and life? Write them down – even if they don't relate to what you think is your gift. You may surprise yourself. For example, I discovered that songwriting and writing books was one of my greatest loves, yet I spent most of my time singing on a platform. When I began to spend more time writing, I experienced a centering and balance that overflowed into my anointing as a public minister.

2. What is your style? Think about the things you love – musical tastes, movies, books – this will give you a good indication of what you are drawn to. Now think about how you minister both publicly or on a personal level. Are you allowing who you are to be released? Or are you trying to do what you think would be most accepted? Allow who you are to flow as you minister. Write down three things about yourself that are uniquely you.

3. What do you know to be true about who God is? Without thinking too much, write down the first word that comes to mind. Then ask yourself, *"Why do I think this about the Lord?"* Does it come from your testimony? Look back over your life to see why you have this revelation about who God is. Now look at how you minister – does it carry this revelation?

Chapter Ten

What to do When you Don't Know What to do

Most of us have had the experience of seeing the Lord moving in a powerful way during a worship time but not really knowing how to partner with that. There have been many times I have been on a platform and felt a shift in the atmosphere and then not known what to do next.

We are never going to have all the answers. But we can learn to read a situation so that we are more strategic and better equipped to step into what the Lord is doing. I like to think of it as being responsible with the gifts the Lord has given me by studying, preparing and spending time with Him. Our focus will always be on loving the Lord and honoring Him and then out of that should flow learning how to host Him during our worship encounters.

We can often think just because something is prophetic, it means that we are not going to know what to do. Yet if the Father is our friend, we can learn to know His heart and personality. This helps us step into an authority only reserved for those closest to Him. He wants to reveal Himself to us. How we partner with that is up to us. The first step in knowing what to do is getting to know Him. The more we know Him, the more confidence we will have to know what He wants and how He wants us to minister in certain situations.

Here are some thoughts for you to consider when you are faced with that moment of not knowing what to do when leading worship:

He wants to reveal Himself.
First and foremost, God is not trying to hide from us. He always wants to reveal Himself. God wants us to know Him. He wants us to be aware of who He is and what He is doing.

Amos 3:7 NKJV
"Surely the Lord God does nothing, unless He reveals His secret to His servants the prophets."

Daniel 2:28 NIV

"...but there is a God in heaven who reveals mysteries."

Amos 4:13 NIV

"He who forms the mountains, creates the wind and reveals his thoughts to man, He who turns dawn to darkness and treads the high places of the earth- the Lord God Almighty is his name."

Proverbs 29:18 MSG

"If people can't see what God is doing, they stumble all over themselves; but when they attend to what He reveals, they are most blessed."

John 14:17 GNT

"He is the Spirit, who reveals the truth about God. The world cannot receive him, because it cannot see him or know him. But you know him, because he remains with you and is in you."

John 16:13 GNT

"When, however, the Spirit comes, who reveals the truth about God, he will lead you into all the truth. He will not speak on his own authority but he will speak of what he hears and will tell you of things to come."

2 Corinthians 2:14 HNV
"But thanks be to God, who always leads us in triumph in Messiah and reveals through us the sweet aroma of his knowledge in every place."

Prayer and worship is a dialogue not a monologue
Don't feel you need to fill up everything with a song. Creating space to listen as well as speak/sing is so important. Don't be afraid of silence. It's ok to have space. We often practice our songs but how about practicing space or silence? I find in the moments of rest and quiet the Lord is willing and ready to speak. Many times He is not speaking because He can't get a word in! We are not having conversation *with* Him, we are talking *at* Him.

Yes, we are singing to bring glory to Him but He longs to respond out of the overflow of His heart as well. He longs to connect with us and speak to us. He is often silent because we don't give Him the space to speak.

I remember leading worship recently where I had this experience. It was so wonderful. I was in the middle of leading a song at a conference when I felt a shift take place.

It was almost like we were at the doors of heaven and then all of the sudden we were in the throne room.

What was most surprising was that the congregation was really in charge – not me. They were really leading the song. I was being carried along by their adoration of Jesus. It was such an amazing time. I remember thinking to myself, *"I'm not really in control here."* And it was wonderful.

Once we came to the end of the song, the band and I were ready to step into the next song, or do *something*! Have you ever had that feeling? You need to do *something*. In that moment I heard the Lord laughing and saying to me, *"You don't have to do anything right now. Just stop and enjoy. I am liking this space. I am enjoying this."* So I put the microphone down and waited – wondering what was going to happen next.

There was about 2-3 minutes of complete silence. Yet it was not awkward or uncomfortable. The air was thick with the presence of love. It was beautiful! Then spontaneously the congregation began to sing out. At first it was quiet and came from different parts of the auditorium, then eventually it was a loud throng of adoring voices lifting up their voices to heaven. This went on for quite some time. In fact, I don't even think we got to the next song. I didn't lead anything. I just stood there! Sometimes leading is getting out of the way. Don't be too concerned about space and silence.

You are probably gathering by now that if we are not listening, as well as leading, we will just go through the motions of leading worship.

If it's not working, move to the next song/section. Don't feel you need to keep playing or singing something over and over unless you have a prompting by the Holy Spirit to do so. If it's not working, move to the next song.

Sometimes we can even get "stuck" in a spontaneous moment that is going nowhere. This can distance people from their worship experience with God. Just let it go and move on. It's ok! We can think that we are singing something that is anointed and as we are doing so, the congregation is disengaging – sitting down, yawning, disconnecting. These spontaneous moments then become a little self-indulgent. The worship team is having a great time but no one else is really understanding what is happening.

In your own personal worship time it's ok to do this but we must always be mindful of the dynamic that we are taking people with us in a corporate setting. What may seem right and natural for us on the platform may not be the best expression for a congregation. I have been in too many worship services where the worship leader is having their own amazing personal worship time with the Lord yet the people are not engaging with them. If you sense this happening, make the change and move to the next song, or next part of the service. Our role is as a servant – we must always minister in a way that encourages others to draw closer to the Lord.

Again, the main focus is on listening, as well as leading.

Allow a musical space: "Selah"
I have always believed that musical instruments can speak. I have often heard a guitarist or a drummer play a musical interlude that was powerful in releasing something during a worship time. If I listen intentionally, I can even get a sense of what the instrument is trying to say. That may seem strange but if you workshop this, you will find that a group of people (*e.g.* in a rehearsal) can often communicate what an instrument is trying to reflect. This certainly takes a sensitivity to listen and lead with your spiritual ears. It means always being alert to what the Lord is trying to communicate.

We should never get up on a platform and go through the motions of looking at chord charts and playing the notes. It is not enough. More is required of us. As you play, every sound is a work of art that has lovingly been tended by you. Don't just let it fly into the air without a target. Use your heart to play your instrument.

Recently I was leading worship from the keyboard at a church. As I was playing, I felt the Lord say to me *"I want everyone to stop playing their instrument and I just want the violin to play over that woman in the third row."* Now, I didn't really want to do this, because the worship had momentum and it was comfortable. The thought of stopping everything and then explaining what we were going to do seemed so clunky to me. I didn't want to ruin the moment! But what seems right in our eyes isn't always God's plan. After a few minutes of "discussion" with Jesus, I asked the whole band to stop playing. I explained that I felt the violin was only meant to play over this woman. I did not know the woman and I really hoped it was not going to embarrass her.

The violinist played over her for about 3 minutes. It was stunning and the anointing was very strong. It was so quiet you could even hear the sound of the wood and the earthiness of the violin as the musician weaved his hands over his instrument. After he finished playing over her, we continued with our worship time.

A few days later I received an email from the pastor. This woman was actually his sister! What I also did not know was that in her younger years, she was studying to be a professional ballerina. She had won a scholarship to go and work overseas and would often dance to classical music. However, during her scholarship she had succumbed to an injury that meant she could not pursue her lifelong dream of dancing. When the violinist played over her – it was similar to the type of music she would dance to. Even though we knew none of this, the Lord knew and it felt like he was showing her that He had not forgotten, that He still remembered the unfulfilled dreams that were in her heart.

Let the congregation know
Sometimes it is completely fitting to let the congregation know that you don't know what to do. This can create an engagement that helps people connect and contribute to what the Lord is wanting.

When I have been in services where I have felt the tangible presence of God affecting people, it can be hard to know how to lead the congregation – mainly because I don't want do anything that hinders His presence moving. I have noted that a service at that moment can go one of two ways: either the leaders on the platform are not aware of their contribution to the Spirit of the Lord moving and just keep going with the run sheet or program; or the alternative is that leaders pause and become aware that God has plans to reveal His love and presence in a tangible way.

What do we do in that moment? What happens next? If we work with the Holy Spirit, He will direct us. He wants to partner with us because He considers us His friend.

In that moment, talk with the Lord. Ask Him questions like:

> *"Lord what are you wanting us to do here?"*
> *"Should I move to the next song? Or should I keep singing the previous song?"*
> *"Should I or someone else on the platform sing something spontaneous"?*
> *"Are you trying to show us something different? Are you trying to teach us something?"*

Sometimes you will find the Lord may respond by asking you to do nothing. That's hard for a leader to do. We think that leading strongly and boldly means we always have to have options. We need to know what to do next. But sometimes the Lord just wants you to be still. I find the Lord likes space. He likes the stillness.

There have also been many times when I haven't had a response at all from the Lord when I have asked these questions! These are the moments when I really don't know what to do. I am beginning to become more comfortable with these moments, because I realize that the Lord wants to do something not just for a group of people but in me. During moments like these, I am learning:

- He wants me to trust Him – will I trust Him when my gifts and talents are not able to take us to the next place in a worship time?

- He wants to show me He is the one in charge, that He really is the worship leader.

- He wants to create space to allow me and others to perceive what is happening in the spirit realm. Moments like this cause us to stop and think and see with spiritual senses. He is training us.

- He is training the worship team to be more sensitive to moves of the Holy Spirit.

And there is so much more.

We don't have to feel that because we are leaders we must have all the answers. However, this thought is different from *not* being a strong leader. You can still lead well, even though you may not know what to do next in a service.

SUMMARY – WHAT TO DO WHEN YOU DON'T KNOW WHAT TO DO

1. God wants to reveal Himself.
2. Worship is a dialogue, not a monologue – the Lord wants to speak to us.
3. Create space and allow instruments to also lead the worship – you don't always have to lead with your voice.
4. It's ok if you don't know what to do – you don't have to have all the answers.

ACTIONS

1. During a rehearsal time or during a worship time, listen with your heart to what the musicians and singers are playing – is there anything that stands out that needs to be brought to the forefront? Sometimes it can be something on the drums, or a solo from a violin. Allow them to play. Be aware of what is happening and create the room for this moment. What do you sense that instrument is trying to say? Afterwards discuss it as a team, or allow time after a service to dialogue with the team.

2. This is a great exercise in seeing how music without lyrics can still convey images and feelings. Choose an instrumental piece of worship music, or a piece of music that has meaning to you. Play this during a team rehearsal or in your personal journaling time. Ask people to write down what they see/feel when they hear this music. At the end, ask everyone to discuss what they saw or felt. Is there a large portion of the group that expressed seeing and feeling the same thing?

3. Think about some very simple ideas you could incorporate that would help take your church into a

new space with God. For example, is it choosing fewer songs in your worship set? Is it allowing an instrument to prophetically play something? Is it having a moment of silence? Reading a scripture? What is something you could incorporate that would help pioneer the new song? Write them down and then discuss.

Chapter Eleven

Different Expressions of Heaven's Song

In this chapter I would like to discuss some different expressions of heaven's song. I am mainly focusing on those that are most used in a corporate gathering but these expressions are also appropriate and effective in your own personal times. There are so many ways we can express the heart of the Father, this is really only just a few of them.

With every expression of heaven's song:

1. We reveal who the Father is and what He does.
2. We remind ourselves and others of the greatness of our God.
3. It allows us to thank Him.

Psalm 30:4 GNT
"Sing praise to the Lord, all his faithful people! Remember what the Holy One has done and give him thanks!"

Davidic/Harp and Bowl worship

No matter what song we release, the banner or the "umbrella" is Davidic, or Harp and Bowl worship. You may have heard these terms before. Before we discuss the different expressions, let me briefly explain what Davidic and Harp and Bowl worship implies.

Combining singing and music with prayer and intercession is where we have coined the terms "Davidic Worship" or "Harp and Bowl" Worship. This worship style happens several times through the scriptures and is also a popular form in movements like IHOP, for example. We can use this worship style to form a basis for different expressions of heaven's song, knowing it has impact over the earth and in heaven and forms its basis from the scriptures.

Davidic Worship

Both in the tabernacle of David and Solomon's temple we see the importance of dance, music and singing as an expression of praise and worship to God. Singers and musicians were appointed around the clock to worship continuously.

Before this, the tabernacle of Moses was where God's glory dwelled. There were distinctive differences between both Moses and David's tabernacle: In David's tabernacle, we see:

- A departure from established worship and praise into more of a spontaneous, free form style.
- Continuous worship.
- A decline of daily animal sacrifice and more focus on the sacrifice of the heart.
- No longer a separation of the people from the presence of God. (In the tabernacle of Moses, The Holy of Holies was separated by a veil and only available to the High Priests).

Then in the book of Acts, God promises He will restore The Tabernacle of David in the end times:

Acts 15:15 -17 NIV
"The words of the prophets are in agreement with this, as it is written: [16] *'After this I will return and rebuild David's*

fallen tent. Its ruins I will rebuild and I will restore it, ^{17} *that the remnant of men may seek the Lord and all the Gentiles who bear my name, says the Lord, who does these things.'"*

Harp and Bowl

Harp and Bowl is a term to signify the combination of worship and intercession.

The idea is taken from the scripture in Revelation 5:8:

Revelation 5:8 NIV
"And when he had taken it, the four living creatures and the twenty-four elders fell down before the Lamb. Each one had a harp and they were holding golden bowls full of incense, which are the prayers of the saints."

The Harp represents worship – the music of heaven – and the golden bowls represents intercession – the prayers of the saints. When we sing the music of heaven, it fills the bowl, thus implying that when we worship in spirit and in truth, we are also interceding. Our worship becomes warfare.

I love how this scripture could imply that the elders were singing and praying simultaneously. They were holding both at the same time.

The four expressions of heaven's song

For the purpose of our study, let's look at what I feel are the four main expressions of heaven's song. These are:

1. The song of thanksgiving.
2. The song of breakthrough.
3. The song of prophetic declaration.
4. The song of love.

1. The song of thanksgiving

Psalm 95:2 NIV
"Let us come before him with thanksgiving and extol him with music and song."

We are admonished in the scriptures to enter into God's presence with thanks and praise. I believe praise is the entry point into His presence.

To release that in song is a great way to release heaven. The Lord loves it when we praise Him. If you long to experience more of God's presence in your life and worship times, praise and thanksgiving is so important. It creates the right setting, one that is fitting for our King.

Psalm 100:4 NIV
"Enter his gates with thanksgiving and his courts with praise; give thanks to him and praise his name."

I love how the *Message* translation says it:

Psalm 100:4 MSG
"Enter with the password: 'Thank you!' Make yourselves at home, talking praise. Thank him. Worship him."

A sacrifice of praise

We read in the book of Jonah that a song of thanksgiving can be given as a sacrifice. What does that mean? It means that even when you don't feel thankful, or things are difficult, we are aware of the greater truth that God is always good and faithful. Regardless of our circumstances we continue to praise Him. Thanksgiving is not determined by our circumstances but by who God is.

> *Jonah 2:9 NIV*
> *"But I, with a song of thanksgiving, will sacrifice to you. What I have vowed I will make good. Salvation comes from the LORD."*

> *Hebrews 13:15 NIV*
> *"Through Jesus, therefore, let us continually offer to God a sacrifice of praise – the fruit of lips that confess his name."*

Characteristics of a thankful song:
1. Expresses who God is.
2. Reveals to us and reminds us of how blessed we are.
3. Full of praise.

Words that describe thanks:
Blessed, grateful, indebted to, honor, respect, overwhelmed, pleased, satisfied.

2. Song of breakthrough

The Merriam-Webster Dictionary describes the word "breakthrough" as:

> *1: an offensive thrust that penetrates and carries beyond a defensive line in warfare;*
>
> *2: an act or instance of breaking through an obstacle;*

A breakthrough anointing cuts through spiritual strongholds to bring freedom and release. Breakthrough words carry a power to vanquish that which has come to destroy. A song of breakthrough slices an atmosphere of oppression and can bring peace, rest and clarity.

A great example of the power of the song of breakthrough is when King Saul, oppressed by an evil spirit, calls for the young David to come and play over him:

1 Samuel 16:23 NIV
"Whenever the spirit from God came upon Saul, David would take his harp and play. Then relief would come to Saul; he would feel better and the evil spirit would leave him."

When you sing a song of breakthrough you carry a sound that shifts the spiritual authority from darkness and turns it over to the light.

Another example can be found in:

2 Chronicles 20:21-22 NIV:
"After consulting the people, Jehoshaphat appointed men to sing to the Lord and to praise him for the splendor of his

holiness as they went out at the head of the army, saying: 'Give thanks to the LORD, for his love endures forever.' [22] *As they began to sing and praise, the LORD set ambushes against the men of Ammon and Moab and Mount Seir who were invading Judah and they were defeated."*

This is such an amazing story – to think that a battle strategy to win a war was to send out the singers first. What is also interesting is the subject matter of their song. They weren't singing "we are going to win this war," or "we are stronger than the enemy." Their focus was on the enduring love of God. In essence they were singing, "We thank God because He has loved us before this moment and He will love us after this moment and because He loves us, we know that we are looked after and protected by Him."

The song of breakthrough does not necessarily have to be directed at a specific situation; it carries breakthrough because we sing of themes that are greater and more powerful than what we are being faced with.

The song of breakthrough is immediate. There is a sudden shift as you sing into a situation that is now. Things can change in a moment. This song carries healing and many people can receive spiritual and physical healing as the song is being sung, just like King Saul did.

Characteristics of a breakthrough song:
1. It breaks through obstacles.
2. It carries themes that bring release but does not always speak into a specific situation.
3. It is immediate.

Words that describe breakthrough:
Release, freedom, discovery, quantum leap, improvement, rise, leap forward, shatter, pull down, cutting edge, progressive.

3. The song of prophetic declaration

At first glance, the song of breakthrough and the song of prophetic declaration can look the same but they are slightly different.

They seem similar because they both carry the theme of warfare on them. To sing both of these expressions you need to be a fighter – you need to be a warrior. You stand up against what is trying to oppress or possess.

Prophetic declaration speaks directly into a specific situation, whereas the song of breakthrough can carry many themes that bring a release without necessarily speaking into a particular situation.

With the song of prophetic declaration, you may also be singing of something that has not yet happened. This also builds faith in those that hear it. Although there may be an immediate change in the spiritual atmosphere, it may be some time before we see the outworking of it.

Here are a few examples from scripture of a song that carries a prophetic declaration:

Numbers 21:17 NIV
"Then Israel sang this song: 'Spring up, O well! Sing about it...'"

Isaiah 26:1 NIV
"In that day this song will be sung in the land of Judah: We have a strong city; God makes salvation its walls and ramparts."

Isaiah 54:1 NIV

"Sing, O barren woman, you who never bore a child; burst into song, shout for joy, you who were never in labor; because more are the children of the desolate woman than of her who has a husband says the Lord."

Revelation 5:9 NIV

"And they sang a new song: 'You are worthy to take the scroll and to open its seals, because you were slain and with your blood you purchased men for God from every tribe and language and people and nation.'"

Characteristics of the song of prophetic declaration:
1. Speaks directly into a specific situation.
2. You may be singing of something that will happen in the future, yet there will still be a change in the atmosphere in that moment.
3. It builds faith in those that hear it and encourages others to believe for what is to come.

Words that describe prophetic declaration:
Affirmation, answer, revelation, statement, authority, divine intervention, foretold, reveal, future speak, unveiled, authoritative, faith-filled, direct.

4. The love song

The song of love expresses our heart for the Father. It is just that, a love song.

Isaiah 5:1 NIV
"I will sing for the one I love a song about his vineyard:
My loved one had a vineyard on a fertile hillside."

I find when I run workshops in releasing heaven's song that the love song is the default position for most people. Most people would find this expression the easiest to release. It is therefore one of the most common forms of heaven's song.

Even though this is the simplest form of releasing heaven's song, it is actually the most difficult to express in a corporate setting. This is because it is very personal in nature, which can sometimes alienate or disengage a congregation.

In your personal worship times your approach in singing a love song in a spontaneous way may be different than in a congregational setting. When I am on my own and my devotional time is between me and the Father, I am a lot more open, personal, and specific with the Lord.

This does not mean I bring "less" in a congregational setting but it does mean I formulate a more appropriate response that includes people, rather than excludes them.

The relationship between a husband and wife will be more intimate when they are alone, yet in a more public setting they can still express that they love each other. This is also like our love song to the Lord – it may look different in a public setting.

Please understand that I am not saying we don't bring our whole hearts when we sing publicly. What I am saying is that we can use unique language that helps us engage and include people. Otherwise it can become performance oriented as people watch instead of join in.

I have been in services where someone begins to sing their love song to the Lord. Although it is beautiful, it is often an exchange between them personally with the Lord. Sometimes this is appropriate but I have found that most times this is very disengaging for a congregation. It can even be boring!

I believe our role in releasing heaven's song is to engage people, to help them connect with heaven. If you are having your own personal time on the platform, it doesn't help anyone else. We should be the "door openers." Whether that means you create moments of heaven's song for people to sing along to, or you create space to minister to them and/or the Lord, our mission is to help those who we are worshipping with to engage with the Lord.

Alone in the secret place however, the love song is *so* powerful. There is such freedom when we just love on Jesus. One of my favorite pastimes is to sing to Jesus about how much I love Him. No agenda, not asking for anything, just loving Him because of who He is.

Expressing the love song to the Lord publicly
If you do feel prompted to sing a love song in a corporate environment, how do you do so in a manner that helps others express their love to the Lord?

Here are some ideas:

1. Choosing simple phrases that people can follow. This immediately allows people to sing with you and includes them in expressing their love to the Lord.

2. Use words like "we, us, our," rather than "I, me and my." A simple example would be changing a phrase from "I love You" to "we love You." There is also power in everyone joining together in agreement as a whole, rather than the emphasis being on their own personal commitment to the Lord.

3. Ask people to sing their own song to the Lord. Have a moment in the service where everyone is singing spontaneously, whether that be in tongues, or during a section of a song, or singing certain lines that they feel prompted so sing. I personally love the sound of everyone lifting their own song up to the heavens. Doing it all at the same time means people can sing more personally and their worship time in a congregational setting can be more intimate.

4. The love song can look different in different congregational settings. For example, how we lead and sing in a prayer meeting, a 24/7 worship event, or a healing meeting, may be different from a Sunday church service. Accommodate the love song depending on the structure and theme of a service.

I once heard a story of a worship leader in Europe who was leading a spontaneous time of worship. He and the band sensed the power of God so strong and were having a wonderful time just expressing their love to the Lord. As he was leading from the stage, he could see his wife at the back of the auditorium glaring at him! He closed his eyes and continued to worship. Every time he opened his eyes and saw his wife, she was staring right at him and didn't look too impressed.

On their way home after the service, he said to her, "Wasn't that the most amazing time of worship?" She nodded her head and remained silent. Finally, he asked her if something was wrong. She turned to him and said, "Don't ever do that again!"

"Do what?" he said.

She responded, "You and the whole band were sitting at the table of the Lord feasting, eating to your heart's content, while the rest of us watched. We were invited to the table to watch you eat. Please don't ever do that again."

Is this what our worship times are like? They shouldn't be. We should be inviting others to the table to eat. How we release and lead will determine this.

Please understand there are no solid rules here. We can't put God in a box. What works for one church family, may not work in another church family. Your role is to always be listening to the heartbeat of heaven to know what is appropriate for the people you are ministering to. If you feel a love song is what is needed, than feel released to do it! But don't do what most worship leaders do and fall back to this style of singing because you don't know what else to do! For it to have impact, it must be expressed well and it must build and bless.

Characteristics of a love song
1. It is very personal, heartfelt and genuine.
2. It is not asking for anything, it is pure adoration because of who He is.
3. Expresses our heart for the Father.

Words that describe love:
Tender, deep affection, beloved, enamored, adore, affection, devotion, loyal, worship, cherish, devoted, delight, heart, care, kindness, friendship.

SUMMARY – DIFFERENT EXPRESSIONS OF HEAVEN'S SONG

HARP AND BOWL/DAVIDIC WORSHIP IS THE UMBRELLA FOR DIFFERENT EXPRESSIONS OF HEAVEN'S SONG

Type of Heaven's Song	Characteristics	Words that describe
Thanksgiving	1. Expresses who God is. 2. Reveals to us who God is. Reminds us how blessed we are 3. Full of praise.	Blessed, grateful, indebted to, honor, respect, overwhelmed, pleased, satisfied.
Breakthrough	1. Breaks through obstacles. 2. Carries themes that bring release but does not always speak of specifics. 3. It is immediate.	Release, freedom, discovery, quantum leap, improvement, rise, leap forward, shatter, pull down, cutting edge, progressive.
Prophetic Declaration	1. Speaks directly into a specific situation. 2. You may be singing of something that will happen in the future, although you will sense a change in the atmosphere in the moment. 3. Builds faith in those that hear it and encourages them to believe for what is to come.	Affirmation, answer, revelation, statement, authority, divine intervention, foretold, reveal, future speak, unveiled, authoritative, faith-filled, direct.
Song of Love	1. Personal, heartfelt and genuine. 2. Not asking for anything, it is pure adoration because of who He is. 3. Expresses our heart for the Father.	Tender, deep affection, beloved, enamored, adore, affection, devotion, loyal, worship, cherish, devoted, delight, heart, care, kindness, friendship.

ACTION

1. Out of the four themes mentioned above, choose one expression that stands out to you. Over a simple chord structure at home, or with a worship team during rehearsal, sing something out.

2. You will notice that I have attached unique words to each expression. This is to give you a leverage point for more ideas. The right language creates the right atmosphere. What are some other words you can think of for each expression? Write them down. Use these words in songwriting and experiment.

3. These are just a few examples. What other expression of heaven's song can you think of? What setting would they be most effective in? What words can you think of that describe them?

Chapter Twelve

How to Turn Spontaneous Songs into Structured Songs

In my earlier years as a songwriter, my most common writing style was to launch out of an inspired hook or lyric (when they came), then craft structure around it. When I began my career at a professional level, there were many co-writing sessions where there was not even inspiration to lead the way. A time would be booked-in and I just had to write, sometimes with people I didn't even know that well. It was a discipline that I am so grateful for and it was also a great experience.

In recent years however, my approach has shifted dramatically. It is not because there was anything wrong with a structured writing style but more so because my gifting has led me to the area of the spontaneous as a new starting point for writing songs. It's just how my gift works best.

I find these days that I lean more towards a more prophetic approach to writing. I find I no longer wait for the inspiration but my "launching pad" is just spending time worshipping the Lord. Out of those moments, I am finding a new foundation for my songs. Themes and ideas pour out of my spirit that I did not even know were there. Once I broke off the shackles of my own restraints and was free to sing from the overflow of my heart, I found there was a lot more inside of me than I had originally anticipated.

Let me just preface by saying that there is nothing wrong with however you feel most comfortable to write. I am just proposing a new approach to invigorate your writing and worship experiences. An anointed song is about the heart before it is about any strategy!

What does it mean to write spontaneously?
- Singing or playing whatever comes out of your heart in times of private or corporate worship times;
- Taking those spontaneous ideas and using them as a basis for a structured song, or using what you have as a completed song.

Why turn them into structured songs?
- To capture what would otherwise be lost or forgotten.
- God-inspired words can continue to be sung and heard over and over again.

Spontaneous moments can be direct downloads from heaven. Coupling that download with the craft of songwriting is a powerful combination.

It is important to know and understand structure. Whether you use it or not is another issue altogether! I firmly believe being a thoughtful, creative, and disciplined worshipper is what opens the doorway of the prophetic. Too many creative people who love the prophetic never refine their gift.

There is nothing I appreciate more than the prophetic voice that understands the scripture and has sound theology, or the prophetic worshipper who understands how to craft a song so that it is memorable and can reach beyond a specific genre or style. It is not one or the other – the spontaneous song and structure can work together well. They are brothers.

Whatever comes out of the overflow of your heart will align with scripture if the word of God has taken root in your spirit and your mind and will be presented well if you have disciplined yourself in the craft of writing. A great combination!

Characteristics of a spontaneous writing style
Some things I have noticed about this type of writing style are:

- The songs are very simple in melody and lyrics.

- They often contain one or two themes – they are not crowded with too many ideas.

- They are sometimes unexpected. You are not looking for a song, you are looking to the one who gives the song. The focus is on Jesus.

- They can come quickly, although afterward it may take time to craft what has been entrusted to you.

If this is something you would like to develop more, here are some ideas I have found helpful:

Start your worship time with a well-known worship song

As you begin to sing to the Lord, sing a song that means something to you or a song that is easy for you to worship to. It may be one of yours, a hymn, or a song that is sung in church. Remember it's important just to relax and enjoy the Lord. Choosing a song that you are comfortable with and that you know well helps you walk into heaven's song. They are popular and heartfelt for a reason! They are heaven's songs as well.

Record

Record *everything*. Whether you are leading worship or you are singing to the Lord at home. Just press record and let it play. Or at least have a recording device available if you step into something.

All our worship times are recorded in our church services because we have a culture of the prophetic song being released. We often like to listen to what we have released and write songs from that. It's a great habit and also helps you to see where there may be stumbling blocks. For example, you may notice as you listen back that the band is overplaying, or there are too many vocalists singing over each other, or there are too many people trying to release the prophetic song. That's how the congregation hears it!

All these things can hinder the song being released to its fullness. There are many dynamics happening in a service that we can be unaware of in the throes of worship.

Listen

Listen back in the car or at home. Sometimes it even helps if it's just on in the background and you are not paying too much attention to it. Just let it fall over you – let it sit with you. I find I am often surprised when I listen back to some things. Sometimes what I think was the main focus isn't what God was highlighting at all. Sometimes what does not necessarily stand out when I am singing really resonates with me as I listen back. This can be because you hear and see things from a different perspective as a *listener* than you would as the *presenter*.

Look for hooks/themes

What stands out to you? Is there a theme or a hook that emerges? Ask the Lord as you are listening to highlight what He wants to highlight. Normally that which attracts your attention is what the Lord is trying to show you is important.

Write out the words

Write the words out. I find using your different senses to take in a song can really help with the songwriting process.

Don't just sing it, don't just listen to it, write it down. Look at the song from different angles.

Choose 3-4 lines that are important

Instead of taking a whole spontaneous experience, choose 3-4 lines, or a section and work around that. Don't think you have to use everything because it was a moment of spiritual download. Sometimes the length of a spontaneous song is more about us trying to climb into what He is really trying to say. It can take us a while to really hear what He is trying to convey.

Is it finished or does it need more work?

Sometimes you may find a whole song from beginning to end comes out of those times. If so, great! I have had moments like this and they are special but rare. They are really amazing and if I knew the formula for that type of song I would give it to you. I really don't know why sometimes it happens like that and why other times I have to search for the treasure that becomes a good song. My advice to you is to be open to either.

Don't be afraid to refine it after you have received it. I meet many people who tell me they don't want to work too hard refining a song if it was given in a prophetic moment. My friend Dan McCollam has a great thought that has really helped me in this area. It comes from the story of the parable of the talents, which is found in Matthew 25:14-30:

Matthew 25:14-30 NIV
"Again, it will be like a man going on a journey, who called his servants and entrusted his property to them. [15] To one he gave five talents of money, to another two talents and to another one talent, each according to his ability. Then he went on his journey. [16] The man who had received the five talents went at once and put his money to work and gained five more. [17] So also, the one with the two talents gained two more. [18] But the man who had received the one talent went off, dug a hole in the ground and hid his master's money. [19] After a long time the master of those servants returned and settled accounts with them. [20] The man who had received the five talents brought the other five. 'Master,' he said, 'you entrusted me with five talents. See, I have gained five more.' [21] His master replied, 'Well done, good and faithful servant! You have been faithful with a few things; I will put you in charge of many things. Come and share your master's happiness!' [22] The man with the two talents also came. 'Master,' he said, 'you entrusted me with two talents; see, I have gained two more.' [23] His master replied, 'Well done, good and faithful servant! You have been faithful with a few things; I will put you in charge of

many things. Come and share your master's happiness!' [24] *Then the man who had received the one talent came. 'Master,' he said, 'I knew that you are a hard man, harvesting where you have not sown and gathering where you have not scattered seed.* [25] *So I was afraid and went out and hid your talent in the ground. See, here is what belongs to you.'* [26] *His master replied, 'You wicked, lazy servant! So you knew that I harvest where I have not sown and gather where I have not scattered seed?* [27] *Well then, you should have put my money on deposit with the bankers, so that when I returned I would have received it back with interest.* [28] *Take the talent from him and give it to the one who has the ten talents.* [29] *For everyone who has will be given more and he will have an abundance. Whoever does not have, even what he has will be taken from him.* [30] *And throw that worthless servant outside, into the darkness, where there will be weeping and gnashing of teeth.'"*

The servant who was given one talent thought he was protecting and entrusting what he had been given to look after but all he was really doing was keeping what he had safe. Two servants found a way to multiply what they had.

It's the same with heaven's song – refining does not necessarily mean you are messing with what God has given you – many times it is *growing* what He has given to you.

What He has entrusted to you is valuable and precious – don't treat it like it's untouchable. It's an investment waiting to grow and multiply.

A song for the people, to the people, or to the Lord

It's not always a song *for* the people or *to* the people. Sometimes we can think the word "prophetic" means you need to give a word to someone. It is so much more than that. Many of my spontaneous songs are simple love songs to the Lord. I wrote the song "With the Angels of Heaven" out of a spontaneous moment of worship. It was one of the few times that almost a whole song came out in complete sections. There are many times as we worship that we are actually hearing what is being sung in heaven and we join with that as we sing out. We may not even realize this is what is happening. Yet this is powerful because as a worshipper, you are releasing the spiritual dimension into the natural dimension.

The song is not always for others to hear

Your moments of spontaneous worship writing may not always be songs for the public. Not every song we write will be for a congregation.

In my experience, there are many reasons why we will receive a download from heaven. Sometimes it's because we are positioning ourselves in such a way that we are hearing what heaven is singing and we replicate that by singing it out ourselves. You are hearing it and so you sing it.

Other times it's for refining and learning. The Lord is trying to teach you what it's like to release heaven's song. I always keep in mind it's for the secret place first before it's for the marketplace. For every song of mine that people have heard, there are many more that are personal or don't translate well to others. Yet at the same time, they are valuable to me and important to me, simply because of the connection I had with the Lord as I sang them out.

Have no agenda – just enjoy God
Have no agenda. The focus is to adore Jesus, not write a song. If nothing spills out, don't get upset or disappointed. I always approach these times as my prayer time and just enjoy what the Lord wants to dialogue with me. If it's just a time where I love on Him and tell Him how wonderful He is, this is not lost time. This is precious. When I hold my little son at the end of the day and I sing him to sleep and kiss his rosy cheeks, I am not hoping for something in return. I do it

because I enjoy it. I just love being his momma. It's the same with the Lord – let's just love being His kids.

I am not meaning this to sound complicated. These are just ideas to help you get started and to grow in your confidence. You may even notice that you are often doing all of these things unconsciously. The key is just to enjoy the process, enjoy the craft and enjoy the creativity of releasing heaven's song.

SUMMARY – HOW TO TURN SPONTANEOUS SONGS INTO STRUCTURED SONGS

1. To write spontaneously means taking what is the overflow of your heart and turning it into a structured song.

2. This helps us to capture what otherwise would be lost or forgotten.

3. It can help to start your worship time with a well-known song.

4. Record everything.

5. Look for hooks/themes.

6. Write out the words.

7. Choose the lines that are important.

8. It can be a song for the people, to the people, or to the Lord.

9. It is not always for the public to hear.

10. Have no agenda – just enjoy it!

ACTION

There have been a lot of ideas mentioned above that you can incorporate but here are a few more ideas to get you started:

1. If there are a few lines or an instrumental hook that you have received during a time of spontaneous release, aim to build a song around it, using the ideas above.

2. If appropriate, present this song during a worship time in a public service, then review with the team how it was received and how it changed the atmosphere.

3. Create a "heaven's song" night, where people can come and present their song in an open mic forum. These can be a lot of fun. You may also find if you only have something small, or only a section of a song, that someone else presenting something small may be able to work together with you to create a complete song together.

Chapter Thirteen

CULTIVATING AN ATMOSPHERE THAT RELEASES HEAVEN'S SONG

There are things we can do and attitudes we can have that attract the presence of God and encourage all of heaven to participate and engage in our worship. That's what I want more than anything and if it means I need to change the way I do things or press in to areas that are new, I will try and do it for the sake of the Lord feeling welcome in my home and worship.

In my experience, here are some things I have noticed in gatherings I have been a part of that helps cultivate an atmosphere for releasing the prophetic – for releasing heaven's song. I am mainly speaking to leaders here, because you are the ones who will be the catalysts for change in your community.

Freedom to make mistakes

No one wants to feel uncomfortable or make others feel uncomfortable. But I can tell you with full confidence that when you begin to create a culture that releases heaven's song, there are going to be some mistakes, or at best, some interesting moments! How you navigate through this both as a leader and as a worship leader is incredibly important.

If your team feels free to stretch themselves and try new things, there are bound to be mistakes. But the advantage of giving permission to trusted worship leaders is that they will also take risks. Every worshipper and every warrior in the stories of the Bible took risks. God expects the same from us too. Risk-takers are not afraid to make mistakes.

I have been a part of too many services where everything is the same year in and year out. Why? Because people don't want to mess with things. They don't want to offend anyone. It's safe, predictable and people are used to it.

If we live like this, we will have nice church services that make people feel good. Everyone will go home feeling like they had a comfortable, feel-good experience in worship. But what if there is more? Are you prepared to lay aside what man expects to hear what the Lord wants from you? Sometimes they are one and the same but sometimes they are not. How will you know if you don't lead with your heart? Finally, how can we try if we don't feel free to make mistakes?

A culture of "no mistakes allowed" means no one will ever step out and lead what is on their heart. They will always default to what they think is appropriate, what their leaders would expect, what the congregation would like.

You may find that there are only a few people you may trust to lead with freedom this way and that's ok. Not everyone is at the same level of growth and faith. It only takes a few people to lead by example to help others grow into this type of culture. That is why I would suggest you take some key people who you know you can trust and who your leaders can trust, to begin to step out a little more.

My story

I want to share with you a time when I made a mistake and what I learned from that experience. In our church we had just began a new service that was primarily focused towards youth. In all our planning meetings I had got the impression that we were not to have long spontaneous times of worship, the music should be fast-moving, full of energy.

During one of these services I was leading and I am embarrassed to tell you that it was awful. I could not sense the presence of God at all and I was leading in my own strength. I was trying very hard to control how the worship was being directed. My heart was in the right place but I was trying to filter everything through my head at the same time.

During the worship I kept thinking how bored I was by the sound of my own voice! I was getting completely distracted by my own inadequacies. I was not focused on the Lord at all.

Then we hit a moment that was totally unexpected. I began to sing the line of the next song. I was not *feeling* anything. I was really going through the motions. I sang the first three words – and then everything changed. Within a couple of seconds, I felt a shift take place that really shook me. God turned up. I then heard the sound of wind come from the back of the auditorium and travel at lightning speed towards me. As it did, the sound escalated, until it hit me hard right in the stomach! As it did, I toppled backwards and then, so shocked by the experience, I began to cry. I then without thinking said in the microphone *"What was that?"* The whole band and the congregation felt it as well. Our spirit, bodies, and minds became completely alert to what the Holy Spirit was doing.

Now you may be thinking to yourselves, *"Roma, this isn't a story about making mistakes, this is amazing!"* Well, let me tell you how the story ends.

After my announcement to the congregation, I then heard the voice of the Lord so strongly. He said, *"You think you know how I move – well I just changed all the rules."* I felt what God was saying to me was not to predict or learn a formula as to how His presence will be expressed. That is what I was doing! I was going through all the motions, using all my experience to get God's attention. And He didn't like it at all.

Then, when I came back to my senses, my next thought after this amazing encounter with the Lord was, *"This was not the brief I was given. This is too spontaneous. I need to change things!"* And so I immediately kept pushing through that song. It was like forcing a toddler to drink castor oil! I ignored that still small voice and kept pushing forward.

Within a moment, the atmosphere shifted back to the way it was before and I am sad to say ended like a funeral dirge!

The next day, I was talking with my senior pastor and the conversation went something like this:

> "Hey Roma, you did really great yesterday but I would love to debrief with you. There was a moment in the worship where I really sensed a shift in the worship and God was really beginning to move. Could you feel it?"
>
> "Well, yeah I did feel it too." I said sheepishly.
>
> "Well that was awesome, but I noticed that instead of creating the space needed to dwell in that space, you kept moving forward and then it seems the moment was lost. Did you feel that as well?"
>
> "Oh, yes I did. It was terrible!"
>
> "Why did you allow that to happen?"
>
> "Well, I remembered the brief you all gave us and I was scared I was doing the opposite, so I just got back into things and tried to do what you asked us to do for this type of service."
>
> My pastor responded, "I understand that. But I am telling you now, if that ever happens again, just go with your heart. Don't worry about what I told you.

Just go with where the Holy Spirit is leading you. If it doesn't work out, we can talk about it afterwards but I want you to try anyway."

Thanks to my amazing pastor and friend Peter McHugh who really helped cultivate a culture where we have had ebbs and flows, great moments, and train wrecks, all because we are lovers of His presence! Now we see an amazing array of color and creativity as we feel free to go where the Spirit leads us.

It's scary but you should try it.

Provide forums other than Sunday services
If the only space you give for the spontaneous is in your Sunday services, you and your team are going to become frustrated pretty quickly. There are a couple of reasons for this:

- Releasing the spontaneous in one worship service is one-dimensional. A great way to develop your gift is to try it in many different forums. For example, the dynamics in a prayer meeting, leaders meeting, Sunday morning, Sunday night, home group, or worship rehearsal are all very different. There are different freedoms you can take that will allow you to explore that are not always evident in one style of service. This also will help you and others explore where your true gifting and authority really lies. Some people are so gifted as prayer and intercession worshippers, some have a breakthrough anointing and so on. Of course, all these different strengths can work in a Sunday service but you often won't find what you are naturally gifted in if you don't have the freedom you can find in different forums.

- As the worship team begins to engage in this style of worship, increasingly people will step out and take risks. It can be quite overwhelming and sometimes the pendulum can even swing too far, with too many people trying to give a prophetic song or play something on their instrument or prophesy. It can become messy and confusing for the congregation and for the team. Everyone trying it out on a Sunday because that's the only time they can express it can even make leaders shut the whole thing down because it can appear confusing.

- You need to find places where people at different stages of their gifting can experiment, grow and mature. A Sunday service is not always appropriate for this.

- As we have mentioned in previous chapters, it does not have to be in a public forum either. What I have learned when I have worshipped in my own personal worship time has developed me to lead a congregation. Try experimenting in many different forums to see where your strengths are and what needs work.

- As a side note, my favorite worshipper is the one who is willing to lead worship at a campus church or home group, just as much as they would lead a large congregation.

Practice being spontaneous

This can seem like two opposing thoughts.

The instrumentalist and vocalist who improvises easily does so because they have practiced improvising. I remember many years ago singing in a jazz band and in rehearsal the band members would say to me, "In this section we are just going to improvise – just scat over the top."

I was terrified because I didn't understand the structure of jazz music in the first place! I was very young and had no understanding of how to "feel" music or experiment vocally.

I was pretty terrible at knowing when to start and stop. Now after years of doing that plus singing on so many different styles of music as a session vocalist and teacher, it is a lot easier. I had to practice improvising.

What you are really practicing is the art of letting things flow out of you. It's a different way of learning. You are not trying to remember words or melodies; you are experimenting and becoming familiar with what it feels like to sing from the overflow of your heart. Learning to move this way helps you understand how the gift manifests itself within you and where your strengths lie.

If you are only trying something new in a public forum, you won't challenge yourself or experiment as much as you probably would like. You need space and time away from the dynamics of a congregational paradigm.

It's like learning a new language. Understanding the idiosyncrasies of speaking a different way takes time before you can speak the language coherently. In a service, your role is to open a gateway to heaven for others to walk into. It requires good leadership and an awareness of spiritual atmospheres.

Singing prophetically is like learning a new language. If in public is the only place you are experimenting with the prophetic, it can be quite overwhelming. You will stay in a place of confinement – you will limit yourself because you don't know enough of the language.

As you become more confident, you will notice you will sing out more. At first what may have seemed embryonic to you will become more formed. You will begin to see more, hear more, and feel more comfortable. As you practice being spontaneous, you will find it will become more natural.

Review

Review is different from critique. Take time to discuss with your team or close leaders what worked and what didn't work. However, this is not a forum where you tell people how bad they were and what they did wrong. That is so destructive. Everything we speak needs to be uplifting and propelling people into their destinies. It doesn't mean you can't be honest but it is important to talk about what is working and what is not in a manner that creates healthy discussion and trust.

Here are some ideas and questions you can ask that can help direct a time of review:

- Always encourage people in their strengths. *E.g.*, "When you took time in between the first and second song it really created space for people to engage with God's presence," or "I loved how you sang out spontaneously with boldness those few lines at the end of the worship time."

- Was there anything you felt didn't work?

- When it wasn't working, what were you thinking/feeling? What made you feel it wasn't working?

- Did you sense a change in the atmosphere as we worshipped together? What was the flavor? (breakthrough, peace, healing, etc).

- Did the team back you up and flow with you? If not, how can we improve in this area?

- What do you think the Lord was trying to say?

- Sometimes things not working can be as simple as not leading effectively. It may be as basic as not giving definite hand signals to direct where you are going, or the team may not feel confident in your leadership. Many times people have led worship and their anointing is incredible but they don't know how to take a team with them. It's important to discuss what may be hindering the flow so that we can host His presence without limitations.

These are just a few ideas. I would suggest these types of discussions be less structured and more relational. Just allow questions and comments to come out of conversation rather than having a "checklist." You will find one question will naturally lead in to another and you will also be keeping relationship at the forefront.

Make time

I understand that in some churches this can be a contention, in particular in a large church where you have several services back to back. I really appreciate this paradigm and the dynamics that come with this. That is why I suggest that providing other forums to release the prophetic song is important. The team can experiment without a time frame.

The one thing I have never been able to dance around is this issue – the prophetic song will take time. Time to develop and time to form during a service or in your personal worship moments.

If the culture in your church is not one of taking long periods of time and space for the spontaneous to be released then find a way somewhere else to release it. It will impact your main corporate services eventually anyway! The worship team becomes developed during these opportunities and is interceding through worship. That changes atmospheres that echo through all areas and events in a church.

I find when I am given a time frame when I am a guest minister that God will always move within the framework of what is given to me. However, this works because I prepare my heart. I have spent time releasing my song to the Lord at other times. This means that when I am not given much time elsewhere, the song has already made its way for me. I feel His favor on my life and when I begin to sing, His presence is there, ready to minister to the people as they praise Him. But it has come because I was prepared beforehand.

When I don't know where I am going and need to use my GPS while driving, it takes me a little longer to get somewhere. I may be unfamiliar with the territory and looking out for which street I need to turn into next. Once I have been to my destination a few times, I no longer need my GPS and I don't have to concentrate so hard about where I am going. I can just enjoy the ride. It can also be a lot quicker to get there!

In my experience the only time when heaven's song is never released during time constraints is when those time frames are bound in tradition or pride – people not wanting change because "that's how it's always been done," or because they don't want to offend anyone. A people with a pure heart and a passion to see Jesus glorified will always see the Lord's presence released in a tangible way.

Understanding time frames

I often get asked the question "We have a time limit on our services/worship times – we can't allow too much space." Or "What do I do if we only have 10-20 minutes of worship?" or "My pastor doesn't like this style of worship – what do I do?" Here are some of my thoughts:

1. God is a God of order. Not all prophetic and spontaneous worship times need to be drawn out and take hours. So if you belong to a church that does not

allow this, don't think that you can't have spontaneous moments or powerful times during your worship. It's all about how you accommodate this during the time that you have.

I find one of the best strategies is not to plan too much. For example, if you have twenty minutes to lead worship, don't try to incorporate six songs into that time frame – that's just too much "information" and not enough space will be created for the Lord to move. If you have a smaller time frame, think of singing fewer songs – two or three would be appropriate for that time frame. Also keep in mind you don't have to do every song that is on your list. I have often only sang one song, or one song and a tag in a shorter time frame, even though there were four songs on my set list. The key here is to go with the flow. It's hard to go with the flow if you have too much to get through.

Song choice is also important. If you don't have much time, choose songs people know or sing spontaneous lines that are easy for people to sing along to. Keep it simple.

I have held many services where there was not much

time – once I was told we had ten minutes! I wanted to be respectful to the leadership and it was out of my hands, so I just enjoyed worshipping the Lord with the time I had. He moved in a powerful way that morning.

2. Different churches have different cultural expressions of worship. We must be mindful and respectful of that. God will work within a culture if they have a heart to know Him. This is different from people being stuck in tradition and not wanting to change. It is about the heart. He will work if we are open to Him. But it will look different in different church cultures.

Choice of language

I remember leading worship for an event where I was told that people were coming from all different churches with a more traditional focus. These people love the Lord, I don't know "better" than them. It's a different expression of worship. When I asked the organizer of the event if I could lead spontaneously, he told me, "People would find that very confronting, so I don't think you should do it." I realized I had used the wrong wording to describe what I felt the Lord wanted to do. As I began leading, the Lord immediately began to speak to me about prophetically singing something. Initially I was afraid to do this because of the conversation I had with the organizer. Yet the Lord kept speaking to me about it. I asked Him to show me the best way to help people engage and He graciously gave me a great explanation to share with the congregation.

I began to share with them about how when we pray, we pray from our hearts. We don't always read words off a page or a screen. In our deepest prayers it can even be tears. Either way, it's spontaneous and a cry from the deepest part of us. I then went on to explain that as a worship leader, I also like to pray – but I use songs to do it. I shared that just as it is completely fitting to pray spontaneously from our hearts, that it is also fitting to do this in song. I shared with them that I wanted to pray for them in song. Then I sang over them for around 6-7 minutes. It was right and fitting and it was received by everyone.

I did not change who I was or how I operated in my gift but I did change how I worded it. I did not use the words "prophetic worship" once! I learned that day that how we communicate what the Lord is wanting to do will be different in different settings, although the expression may be the same. The language we use is a huge contributing factor to how people receive in moments of spontaneous worship

Be the change you want to see

Sometimes what is most required is that God wants to bring change. There's just no way around it. He brings His order to mess up our order. He wants time. Maybe you are the person who is needed to bring the change that is needed in your congregation.

I have always believed that the worshippers and songwriters are catalysts for change. In some ways we are the pioneers. If you think about church movements in history, they are often marked by their songs. Most people would know "Amazing Grace," "How Great Thou Art," and more contemporary songs like "How Great is our God," "Shout to the Lord" and "The Heart of Worship." These songs have carved out revelations that have permeated most church cultures.

Why would we expect anything less when we lead worship or write songs? We can often think it is fitting for people like Chris Tomlin or Darlene Zschech to be the pioneers and they are – but how about you?

If you want to be led by the Holy Spirit as a worship leader/songwriter, it's not going to be easy sometimes. You may not be understood, you may not be appreciated, you may get things wrong, you may even lose a few friends. Pioneers are going where other people have not gone. They have not gone there for a reason! It's hard work. There will be opposition and it will require patience and steel strength at times. I hope this will not stop you from rising up to be the change that is needed in your church community.

Remember, if everything is done with love and relationship as a focus, you will build and bless. Love the people you are serving and only be silent if the Lord is telling you to be.

Release others

A culture that releases and believes in others is the one that Jesus loves. Be someone else's biggest fan. See the potential that is on the inside of them and help to raise them up into their future.

If we spent as much energy releasing others to release heaven's song as we do promoting ourselves and our own ministry, church would look a whole lot different. I believe with all my heart that God releases those who release others. The freedom and atmosphere that brings is unstoppable and immeasurable. It creates a culture where the Lord can move freely and openly, in and upon whom He wishes.

Find your own identity – every church is different

The release of heaven's song has a different flavor upon those it rests upon. The combination of you and God is unique.

Some things that can shape heaven's song in your church are:

- Its *history* – where the church has come from, denominational background, what it is founded upon.

- Its *destiny* – the mandate and promise, the expectation from heaven for its influence on the region and the nation.

- Its *demographic* – The mix of people and people groups.

Learn from others you respect and love but don't try to be like them. Be like you. Let the song flow out of you as you experience the freedom to be yourself.

SUMMARY – Cultivating an Atmosphere That Releases Heaven's Song

To cultivate a culture of releasing of heaven's song:

1. Allow freedom to make mistakes.
2. Provide forums other than Sunday services.
3. Practice being spontaneous.
4. Review.
5. Make time.
6. Release others.
7. Find your own identity.

ACTIONS

1. To help you understand your identity and your churches identity, here are some questions to ask yourself/discuss as a team. If this still leaves you feeling unsure, observe your church and your worship for a few weeks. It should become evident.

   - What is the history of the church? Is it a new church plant, if so, what was it birthed from?

   - What is your background – what is your testimony? (Think on what is good – if the only memorable history is your salvation story, then build on that).

   - What is the vision of the church?

   - How can the worship reflect this legacy and still move forward into all God has called you to? Or is it time for a new vision or an extension of the vision?

   - What is God calling you to, or what is the corporate destiny of the church?

- What are some of the prophetic words that have been spoken over you and/or the church? Write them down in point form.

- What demographic do you minister to? Is it youth, families? Is it middle class or the homeless? Is it people from a certain nation? Sometimes this can be as simple as what you are drawn to. Who are the people you feel most at home with?

- What are the strengths of these demographics? What is needed?

2. A great exercise is to write a vision down that expresses who you are. This is a lot of fun and a great way to cultivate a culture that released heaven's song.

I am including my vision here to give you an idea of what you can write down. I took parts of prophetic words that were spoken over me that really resonated with me and turned them into a declaration that I can speak out. It reminds me of who God says I am and what He says I can achieve. This vision is different from your mission statement, it is a declaration of who you believe God has called you to be.

MY DREAM FOR MY LIFE

I am a person who has dreams about being in the throne room and to be taken up into the third heaven.

He is pleased to give me entry into His throne room.

This is where it all starts.

To stand in the presence of Angels and to hear worship and have my heart altered in heaven so when I play and sing on Earth, heaven will come down to my playing and to my singing.

They are going to be songs that set the captives free.

They are going to be songs David sang over Saul and brought release to demons.

God is giving me a miraculous song that's going to set people free – it is my life song.

It is a song that launches me into the record books of God's blessing.

He is anointing me with a new "flavor" – not a sound, or fragrance but flavor.

He is giving me a new level of teaching and equipping.

I can stop wondering and be the wonder.

I can embrace who I am in peace and rest.

The water level is rising in my life.

I don't need to fight for it, it has started fighting for me.

I am one of God's messengers, releasing heaven's song across the earth.

Conclusion

You have been presented with a challenge to step into the destiny that God has for you as a worshipper. I hope this workbook has provided forums for you and your teams to grow into your own style and flavor in releasing heaven's song. Remember these are ideas to get you started – you will create your own story! My prayer for you is that as you apply some of the ideas covered here you will step into the dimension that releases new songs, new words, new visions, stories and culture where you live.

It's time to stop looking at the person standing next to you as the person who is going to release something great. My friend, it is you. You have been called. Discover all you were born to be and achieve while on this planet. For in a short time we will be entering heaven's gates and starting a whole new story. Use this short time on Earth to be the worshipper God has created you to be. You can do it!

Printed in Great Britain
by Amazon